When You Get Into Trouble,
Nurse From
Your Holy Qur'an

Pastoral & Spiritual Self-Help For Muslims

Volume One:

ALLAH (GOD),
The Believer, & Suffering

By Demetric Muhammad

Special Thanks And Gratitude

se Is Due To Allah Who Came In The Person Of Master W. Fard
mad.

the Honorable Minister Louis Farrakhan for his great love,
e and noble example of manhood, spirituality, nurturing,
obedience and strength. I can never thank Allah enough for him
at he has meant in helping me find my purpose in life.

to my wife Tomiko, my children Khadir, Bilal and Elisha.

to Brother Student Minister Anthony for his mentorship,
e and example of suffering and winning.

Love and Gratitude to my mother Marilyn and my father David.

Love and Brotherhood to Brother Alan Muhammad, Brother
Muhammad, Brother Jackie Muhammad and Brother Dr. Ridgely
mad.

and Gratitude to Brother Student Minister Robert Muhammad of
Texas, Brother Student Minister Rodney Muhammad of
phia Pennsylvania, Student Minister Ava Muhammad of
Illinois, and Brother Student Minister Abdul Arif Muhammad.
appreciate your encouragement, expertise and fellowship.

and Gratitude to Sister Vivian X Lee for diligent proofing,
and layout. You are peerless in your work, care and speed.

to Ms. Kina Foreman for typing help and technical assistance.

ppreciative to Brother Joe Muhammad of New York, NY;
Marticus Muhammad of Memphis, TN; Brother Jason
mad of Chicago, IL; Brother Bridge Muhammad of Holly
MS; Brother Kendrick Muhammad of
lte, NC; Brother John 8X of Philadelphia, Pa; Brother Student
r Jamil Muhammad of Washington, D.C. Thank you for your

support and help to get this project to the printer and for your moral support.

Thank you Brother Ilia Rashad Muhammad, Brother Andre Muhammad, Brother Derrick 4 Muhammad and Student Captain Anthony J. Muhammad all of Memphis, TN, and Brother Jesse Muhammad of Houston, TX. Special Thanks to Sister Kim Muhammad of Chicago IL for help with cover and Brother Jahleel Muhammad of Detroit, MI for brilliant cover design work

TABLE OF CONTENTS

INTRODUCTION

In The Name of Allah,
the Beneficent, the Merciful

The Holy Qur'an, which is the book of scripture of the Muslims,
 vilified as a text of terror in the modern age of East versus West.
 am continues to grow and is often cited as the fastest growing
 in America and the world. And be it rather through conversion
 r population expansion, the growth of Islam finds Muslims
 home in historically non-Muslim lands.

This book is an effort at providing a clear, concise and simple
 care resource for both Muslims (neophyte and seasoned) and
 uslims. It will be of particular value to Muslims who require
 and spiritual care arising from conditions of discrimination,
 ce and hatred in a post 9/11 world. It will also be beneficial for
 s as they move through the natural vicissitudes of life
 ering, adversity, pain, marital problems, parental problems,
 ic woes, inter-personal dramas and career frustration. This book
 dication for the value, worthiness and utility of the Holy Qur'an
 its critics. This vindication is brought about by this volume's use
 matic study of the Holy Qur'an and the subsequent extraction of
 s of guidance, pearls of pastoral care, and treasure of eternal
 In Islam, Allah is known to have 99 Attributes or Names. The
 ur'an also has attributes or names. One of those names is Al-Shifa,
 s translated as meaning *The Healing*. This volume intends to give
 eliever in Islam the power to use the Holy Qur'an as a book of
 spiritual and emotional healing. For when man and woman enter
 ntal, spiritual and emotional well-being, there is what follows of
 omic, physical and moral well-being as well. In other words, if
 r person comes into harmony with the guiding spiritual principals
 Creator, the outer person can come into harmony with and gain
 of the Creator's creation and enjoy a life of joy and success.

But this volume is also of benefit to the numerous doctors, nurses, teachers, employers, counselors, chaplains and other care providers who find themselves more and more being responsible for Muslim populations. Therefore, this volume does not make any judgments with respect to the various sects or ideologies now resident within the mosaic of Muslims in America or around the world. The goal of this volume is that every believer in the truth of Allah's (God's) revelation of the Holy Qur'an will find use for such a collection of important and powerful Qur'anic ayats (verses). It is interesting to me that most people, Muslim and non-Muslim, have on instant recall song lyrics, words from their favorite movies, or slang street sayings, but are often very limited in their ability to recall verses from the book that many say they would fight to protect. What is even more concerning is that the songs, movies, and cultural slang in vogue today is often comprised of words that contain ideas and philosophies that are in direct opposition to the spiritual teachings of the Holy Qur'an or Bible. So when difficult times emerge in the life of otherwise faithful men and women, there is nothing in their memory banks that they can make a withdrawal from and put into their service as guidance from the divine. This volume's collection of Qur'anic ayats from the English translators of the Holy Qur'an hopes to help all who want to make deposits into their consciousness of what all Muslims believe is Allah's Supreme Wisdom - the Holy Qur'an.

The Qur'an describes itself as being like the honey produced by the honeybee. It is a "drink of various hues" and "a healing for men." This could refer to the Holy Qur'an being comprised of the best of all previous divine prophetic revelations to the various communities of the human family. Allah says in the Holy Qur'an that He has mentioned some prophets in the Qur'an and some He has not mentioned, but divine revelation has nonetheless been the gift of every nation and people. And the best and the eternal parts of all those prophetic traditions can be found within the Holy Qur'an. This aspect of the Qur'anic teaching is the license and tool for Muslims to take a very liberal view of the religious landscape of humanity. It permits Muslims to engage wisdom and truth from wherever it is found, knowing full well that Allah (God) is the ultimate source of wisdom and truth. He is in His attributes al-Hakim (the Wise) and al-Haqq (the Truth), and therefore all wisdom and truth ultimately come from Him even if it is being spoken from the mouth of a parrot (smile). So while the meat of this volume is the verbatim ayats of the Holy Qur'an, this volume will also be adorned with wisdom and truths in the form of wise sayings and quotes from a variety of sources that resonate with the intended audience. If it is true and is in harmony with the precepts and principles articulated in the Holy Qur'an we will take license to employ it as a didactic and pedagogical tool to help what is sometimes the strong medicine of the Qur'anic language, to be digested easier. Of particular utility will, again, be sources that are familiar Muslims in America. This includes hadiths of Prophet Muhammad (pbuh), sayings from the indigenous African-American Muslim tradition, quotes from the Torah and the Gospel, and popular culture references.

It is our prayer to Allah that all Muslims and Muslim care-providers will enjoy this volume and deem it a valuable resource and addition to your toolbox of learning and faith.

Best Wishes.
As Salaam Alaikum.
Demetric Muhammad
December, 2011

The Holy Qur'an is the Muslim Book of Scripture. It contains the words of Allah (God) that were revealed to Prophet Muhammad (saw) more than 1400 years ago. There is a saying familiar in the Muslim community that says: "When you want to talk to Allah, say your prayers. When you want Allah to talk to you, read your Holy Qur'an." The chart on the next page demonstrates the various attributes or names of the Holy Qur'an. Like the 99 Attributes or Names of Allah (God), they demonstrate the rich nature and character of the book. These attributes also list the various functions and uses of this divine revelation. Our beginning to utilize this book as a book of spiritual self-help starts with becoming acquainted with the attributes and nature of the Holy book.

ATTRIBUTES OF THE HOLY QUR'AN
(Excerpt from M. M. Ali English Translation)

No.	Attribute	Meaning	Surah:Ayat
1.	Al-Kitab	The Book; complete in itself	2:2
2.	Al-Furqan	That which Distinguishes truth from falsehood	25:1
3.	Al-Dhikr	The Reminder; source of eminence and glory	15:9
4.	Al-Mauizah	The Admonition	10:57
5.	Al-Hukm	The Judgment	13:37
6.	Al-Hikmat	The Wisdom	17:39
7.	Al-Shifa	That which Heals	10:57
8.	Al-Huda	That which Guides	72:13
9.	Al-Tanzil	The Revelation	26:192
10.	Al-Rahmat	The Mercy	2:105
11.	Al-Ruh	The Spirit; or that which gives life	42:52
12.	Al-Khair	The Goodness	3:104
13.	Al-Bayan	That which Explains all things; clear statement	3:138
14.	Al-Nimat	The Favor	93:11
15.	Al-Burhan	The Clear Argument; manifest proof	4:174
16.	Al-Qayyim	The Maintainer or Rightly-directing	18:2
17.	Al-Muhaimin	The Guardian	5:48
18.	Al-Nur	The Light	7:157
19.	Al-Haqq	The Truth	17:81
20.	Habl-Allah	The Covenant of Allah	3:103

ESSAYS

THEOPHANY, THEODICY AND ESCHATOLOGY

"The Coming of God and The Suffering of The Righteous At The End of Satan's World"

Bismillah Ir- Rahman Ir- Rahim

Theophany

The Most Honorable Elijah Muhammad taught us the knowledge and the Knowledge of Self. The main component of His teaching Knowledge of God was that of the Coming of God.

... in point No. 12:

BELIEVE that Allah (God) appeared in the Person of ...ter W. Fard Muhammad, July, 1930; the long-awaited "...ssiah" of the Christians and the "Mahdi" of the Muslims.

BELIEVE further and lastly that Allah is God and besides ...M there is no god and He will bring about a universal ...ernment of peace wherein we all can live in peace together.

The Holy Qur'an, contrary to popular belief, backs up the ...gs of the Most Honorable Elijah Muhammad (emphasis added):

...10 They wait for naught but that *Allah should come to them* *...he shadows of the clouds with angels*, and the matter has ...ready) been decided. And to Allah are (all) matters returned.

...22 And *thy Lord comes with the angels, ranks on ranks.*

...2 He it is Who caused those who disbelieved of the People of ...e Book to go forth from their homes at the first banishment. ...u deemed not that they would go forth, while they thought ...t their fortresses would defend them against Allah. But *Allah* *...e to them from place they expected not and cast terror into* *their hearts* - they demolished their houses with their own hands and the hands of the believers. So take a lesson, O you who have eyes!

16:33 *Await they aught but that the angels should come to them or that thy Lord's command should come to pass.* Thus did those before them. And Allah wronged them not, but they wronged themselves.

Not only does the Holy Qur'an speak of the coming of Allah but it says that he is visible.

The Holy Qur'an reads in Surah 57 Ayat 3:
Huwa *l-awalu* *wal-ākhiru* *wal-zāhiru* *wal-bātinu* wahuwa *bikulli shayin Aalīmun* (transliteration)

He is the First and the Last and *the Manifest and the Hidden*, and He is Knower of all things. (Maulana Muhammad Ali Translation)

He is the first/beginning and the last/end, and *the apparent/visible, and the hidden/inside*, and He is with every thing knowledgeable. (Ahmed Ali Translation)

He is the first, and the last; *the manifest, and the hidden*: And He knoweth all things. (Sale Translation)

In the original Arabic, the word that is translated into English as *manifest* comes from the Quranic Arabic root word *zahara* that has the following meaning according to the Dictionary of the Holy Qur'an by Omar:

zahara

To appear, become distinct, clear, open, come out, ascend, be manifest, mount, get the better of know, distinguish, be obvious, conspicuous, come forth, go out, have the upper hand over wound on the back, enter the noon, neglect. To help, back, support in the sense of collaboration.

This idea of the coming of God, visible, manifest and apparent is common in the field of religious studies. It is called Theophany. The Holman Bible Dictionary entry for the word Theophany reads as follows:

theophany

Physical appearance or personal manifestation of a god to a person.

Need for a theophany: The basic postulate here is that to see God could be fatal. "He said, "You cannot see My face, for no man can see Me and live!"" (Exodus 33:20 NAS; compare Genesis 16:13; Exodus 3:2-6; Exodus 19:20-21; Judges 6:22-23; Judges 13:20-22.) Yet the record is unmistakable that people did see God, such as Moses and others at Sinai (Exodus 24:9-10); the Lord's rebuke of Aaron and Miriam (Numbers 12:4-8); and the majestic vision to Isaiah (Isaiah 6:1,Isaiah 6:5). Customarily, God is not revealed to ordinary sight, God at times chooses to reveal Himself in theophanies.

Kinds of theophanies. In human form: Without question, the theophany in Exodus 24:10 involved the appearance of a human being, for the text clearly states that a pavement of sapphire appeared "under His feet." At Peniel, Jacob testified that he had seen God face-to-face. (Genesis 32:30). On Mount Horeb, it was the experience of Moses to speak to God "face to face, just as a man speaks to his friend." (Exodus 33:11 NAS). In the same passage when Moses begged God to show him His glory (Exodus 33:18), the Lord graciously granted Moses a vision of Himself, saying, "I will take My hand away and you shall see My back, but My face shall not be seen" (Exodus 33:23 NAS). If it is protested that the subject is enveloped in mystery, it needs to be remembered that theology without mystery is sheer nonsense. God in His wisdom does not restrict Himself to one method of self-revelation. Notice God's pronouncement in Numbers 12:6-8, which was quite unlike that of Deuteronomy 4:12-15 where only a voice was granted.

The Holy Qur'an goes further to acknowledge that the believers will meet their Lord. In fact there are at least 15 passages in the Holy Qur'an that address the meeting with Allah. Below is a sampling of these verses. Other verses on this theme of the Holy Qur'an appear later on in this book.

33:44 Their salutation on *the day they meet Him* will be, Peace! And He has prepared for them an honorable reward.

6:154 Again, We gave the Book to Moses to complete (Our blessings) on him who would do good, and making plain all things and a guidance and a mercy, so that they might *believe in the meeting* with their Lord.

13:2 Allah is He who raised the heavens without any pillars that you can see, and He is established on the Throne of Power, and He made the sun and the moon subservient (to you). Each one runs to an appointed term. He regulates the affair, making clear the messages that you may be certain of the meeting with your Lord.

84:6 O man, thou must strive a hard striving (to attain) to thy Lord, until thou meet Him.

When we go behind the English translation to investigate this theme in the Arabic, we find that the Arabic word *mulaqu* is the word translated into English as *meet*. *Mulaqu* is a form of the Arabic root word *laqiya*. Its meaning in the Dictionary of the Holy Qur'an is as follows:

laqiya

To meet, meet with, see, come across, experience, suffer from, occur, undergo, endure, find out a thing, lean upon, receive, come face to face, go in the direction of or towards.

Based upon this definition we understand that meeting with your Lord implies a difficulty factor. Allah (God) is always described in geospatial terms as being *above*. Surah 90 describes the journey to meet with your Lord as an uphill journey. When we travel up, whether it is a hill, mountain or airplane flight, we are breaking the gravitational pull that inclines us to the earth's surface. This upward travel causes us to experience a change in the atmosphere and the higher we go we eventually encounter fire. The fire of the earth's atmosphere, which results from pure oxygen, is symbolic of the pain involved in *meeting with your Lord.*

We understand this because the Honorable Elijah Muhammad said that what is true on the physical plane is true on the spiritual plane as well. This takes us to the subject of theodicy.

Theodicy

Theodicy is a area of religious studies that deals with the origin of pain and evil and where scholars wrestle with answering the question, 'Why do bad things happen to good people?' When God comes, as it is prophesied, there would be believers and disbelievers in Him. Those who believe have an experience that involves failure, adversity, perseverance, patience, persistence, endurance and faith. The one word and concept that best embodies all of these factors is ***suffering.***

Eschatology

The timing of God's coming fits into a field in religious studies known as Eschatology or End Time prophecies.

The Bible has much to say about the end times. Scholars say that 2/3 of the New Testament is Eschatology and 25% to 30% of the entire Bible deals with the end times.

God comes to reveal the man of sin, the son of perdition, the one marked for destruction, at the end of the workings of Satan. (2Thess. 3-9)

Satan had a work. The Qur'an describes his work as that of pursuing Man from before him, from behind him, from the left and from the right. The Bible describes his work as bruising the heel of the seed of Adam and Eve. He is the great Arch Deceiver whom God's coming is to destroy completely!

Joel 2:11 and 2:31 describe God's coming as a great and dreadful day. Habakkuk 3 describe God's coming as "burning coals went forth at his feet, the tents of Cushan were in affliction and the curtains of the land of Midian did tremble."

Matthew 13:50 describes wailing and gnashing of teeth. But possibly the best description of the End Times is in the Bible's 2Timothy 3, where the condition of the people is detailed and described, and 19 spiritual diseases are revealed:

"You should know this, Timothy, that in the last days there will be very difficult times.
1. For people will love only themselves
2. and their money.
3. They will be boastful and proud,
4. scoffing at God,
5. disobedient to their parents,
6. and ungrateful.
7. They will consider nothing sacred.
8. They will be unloving
9. and unforgiving;
10. they will slander others and
11. have no self-control.
12. They will be cruel and
13. hate what is good.
14. They will betray their friends,
15. be reckless,
16. be puffed up with pride, and
17. love pleasure rather than God.
18. They will act religious, but they will reject the power that could make them godly. Stay away from people like that!
19. They are the kind who work their way into people's homes and win the confidence of vulnerable women who are burdened with the guilt of sin and controlled by various desires. (Such women

are forever following new teachings, but they are never able to understand the truth.)"

Again, those who believe have an experience that involves adversity, perseverance, patience, persistence, endurance and he one word and concept that best embodies all of these factors *ring*. Within the pages of the Holy Qur'an the concept of ng described by any 6 forms of the classical Arabic root word Consider the meaning of three of its forms found in the ary of the Holy Qur'an:

isa To be wretched, miserable, unhappy, destitute, bad, evil.
sun (n.): Terror; Punishment; Harm; Power; Violence; ersity; Conflict; War.
sa (n.): Distress; Adversity; Sorrow; Tribulation; War; lence; Mighty power; Kind of evil that relates to property, h as poverty.
is Poor; Needy; Unhappy.

A major section and arguably the most powerful and important of this book includes the verses of the Holy Qur'an that constitute iversal and significant theme of suffering. A sample of those r ayats are as follows:

4 We have certainly created man to face difficulties.

77 It is not righteousness that ye turn your faces Towards east Vest; but it is righteousness (177) - to believe in Allah (178) the Last Day, and the Angels, and the Book, and the ssengers; to spend of your substance (179), out of love for n, for your kin, for orphans, for the needy, for the wayfarer, those who ask, and for the ransom of slaves; to be steadfast prayer (180), and practice regular charity; to fulfill the tracts which ye have made; and to be firm **and patient (181), ain (or suffering) and adversity**, and throughout all periods anic. Such are the people of truth, the Allah-fearing.

2:214 Or do ye think that ye shall enter the Garden (of bliss) without such (trials) as came to those who passed away before you? They encountered **suffering and adversity**, and were so shaken in spirit that even the Messenger and those of faith who were with him cried: "When (will come) the help of Allah." Ah! Verily, the help of Allah is (always) near!

6:42 Before thee We sent (messengers) to many nations, and We afflicted the nations with **suffering and adversity**, that they might learn humility. (43). When the **suffering** reached them from us, why then did they not learn humility? (861). On the contrary their hearts became hardened, and Satan made their (sinful) acts seem alluring to them.

A close reading of the scripture reveals three primary sources or types of pain or suffering.

1. Satan's Opposition To Man

12:5 He said: O my son, relate not thy dream to thy brethren, lest they devise a plan against thee. The devil indeed is an open enemy to man.

17:53 And say to My servants that they speak what is best. Surely the devil sows dissensions among them. The devil is surely an open enemy to man.

35:6 Surely the devil is your enemy, so take him for an enemy. He only invites his party to be companions of the burning Fire.

36:60 Did I not charge you, O children of Adam, that you serve not the devil? Surely he is your open enemy.

2:36 But the Devil made them slip from it, and caused them to depart from the state in which they were. And We said: Go forth, some of you are the enemies of others and there is for you in the earth an abode and a provision for a time.

41:36 And if a false imputation from the devil afflict thee, seek refuge in Allah. Surely He is the Hearing, the Knowing.

2. Allah's Afflicting The Believers With Testing

6:112 And thus did We make for every prophet an enemy, the devils from among men and jinn, some of them inspiring others with gilded speech to deceive (them). And if thy Lord pleased, they would not do it, so leave them alone with what they forge.

4:78 Wherever you are, death will overtake you, though you are in towers, raised high. And if good befalls them, they say: This is from Allah; and if a misfortune befalls them, they say: This is from thee. Say: All is from Allah. But what is the matter with these people that they make no effort to understand anything?

7:131 But when good befell them they said: This is due to us. And when evil afflicted them, they attributed it to the ill-luck of Moses and those with him. Surely their evil fortune is only from Allah, but most of them know not.

33:17 Say: "Who is it that can screen you from Allah if it be His wish to give you punishment or to give you Mercy?" Nor will they find for themselves, besides Allah, any protector or helper.

2:155 And We shall certainly try you with something of fear and hunger and loss of property and lives and fruits. And give good news to the patient.

3. Suffering From The Consequences Of Our Own Wrong

30:41 Corruption has appeared in the land and the sea on account of that which men's hands have wrought, that He may make them taste a part of that which they have done, so that they may return.

17:13 And We have made every man's actions to cling to his neck, and We shall bring forth to him on the day of Resurrection a book which he will find wide open.

4:79 Whatever good befalls thee (O man), it is from Allah, and whatever misfortune befalls thee, it is from thyself. And We have sent thee (O Prophet) to mankind as a Messenger. And Allah is sufficient as a witness.

6:120 And avoid open sins and secret ones. Surely they who earn sin will be rewarded for what they have earned.

Allah says in the Holy Qur'an that
He is the patron of the believers.

So we have seen that there is vindication to the Honorable Elijah Muhammad's teachings within the classical Islamic tradition. We are seeing that the Quranic Arabic language is our friend in supporting his positions with respect to the reality of Allah (God), the coming of Allah (God) and the dangerous events of the end times. We now take up Allah's merciful response to the believers who come to faith during this, the worst of times in world history.

Allah says in the Holy Qur'an that He is the Patron of the believers. The word patron as used in the Holy Qur'an is 'Maula.' It means:

Maula Patron; Friend; Owner; Master; Protector; Benefactor. It is from the root **Waliya:** To be close, near, follow, be up to.

From this aspect of Allah's nature we get the attribute *Wali*, which means specifically *the protecting friend*. This was one of the names of Master Fard Muhammad. And it is from this that we get the role that Allah plays in the life of the believers. From a formulaic point of view we can say that there are four principle functions of Allah as Patron of the believers.

1. Allah grows the believer from stage to stage.

84:19 That you shall certainly ***ascend to one state after another***.

84:20 But what is the matter with them that they believe not.

Allah placed Adam in a garden. Islam is filled with garden symbolism. Heaven in Islam is frequently described as a garden (*jannah*). The Most Honorable Elijah Muhammad said that heaven is not a place of rest but of work. This garden symbolism is significant because a garden is a place of beauty, benefit, bounty and blessing that comes from hard work and labor. In the call to prayer the muezzin recites *"Hayya ala falah, Hayya ala falah."* This means come to cultivation that leads to success. The word *falah* comes from the Arabic root word *falaha*. According to the Dictionary of The Holy Qur'an by Omar it means:

falaha

To till (the earth), cleave (a thing). Aflaha: To be successful, lucky, live on. Falah: Prosperity; Safety; Success - both in this life and in the hereafter; To unfold something in order to reveal its intrinsic properties, till and break open the surface of the earth and make its productivity powers active. The English word "plough" seems to have been derived from it. It is one of the striking beauties of the Arabic that its words in their primary sense denote the state which when realized, convey the import of the same. This is well illustrated in the word Falah. Falah not only means success but also signifies what constitutes real and complete success. Falah, therefore, consists in the working out of our latent faculties to our best ability, whatever of noble and good hidden in us must come out and what ever is in the form of potentiality in human mind must be converted into actuality. So Falah is really to work out our own evolution and to bring to realization what our Creator has placed in us. Falah is of much higher stage than the attainment of Najah (-salvation). In Arabic language there is no better word than Falah, to describe the attaining what one desires, reaping the fruits of labour, and for success and gains as others may envy, be it material or spiritual, of this world or of the hereafter. Muflih: One who is prosperous, happy.

ordains a way out for the believer.

Allah promises in Surah 65 Ayat 2-3 that He will ordain a way distressful situations for the believers. This is a great comfort to that Allah has planned out our deliverance.

65:2 So when they have reached their prescribed time, retain them with kindness or dismiss them with kindness, and call to witness two just ones from among you, and give upright testimony for Allah. With that is admonished he who believes in Allah and the Latter day. And whoever keeps his duty to Allah, **He ordains a way out for him,**

65:3 And **gives him sustenance from whence he imagines not.** And whoever trusts in Allah, He is sufficient for him. Surely Allah attains His purpose. Allah indeed has appointed a measure for everything.

What is even more reassuring for the believer is that Allah gives sustenance from Himself that will come to us from places that not imagined. We often make our own calculations with regard how we will overcome a challenge within our life or the lives of loved ones. And despair results when we are unable to see clearly what we need is going to come from. These are the greatest verses promised deliverance that I have ever read because these verses acknowledge our own inability to imagine Allah's limitless ability to

From these ayats we take away two powerful and fundamental Allah orders the means by which we are to escape our encounter suffering and Allah suffices our needs in ways that we have not previously considered.

sends angels to help the believers.

Angels are powerful beings who carry out special assignments Allah (God). For us, the most common beings we encounter are our human beings. And we can bear witness to the angelic presence of certain men and women who come into our life to help us in very important and critical ways. Consider the following ayats.

> 41:30 Those who say, Our Lord is Allah, then continue in the right way, **the angels descend upon them**, saying: Fear not, nor be grieved, and receive good news of the Garden which you were promised.
> 41:31 We are your friends in this world's life and in the Hereafter, and you have therein what your souls desire and you have therein what you ask for.

> 41:32 A welcome gift from the Forgiving, the Merciful.

As a student of the Honorable Minister Louis Farrakhan, I don't subscribe to a view of angels as ethereal spirit beings who belong to the realm of the invisible. Instead I see them as men and women deputized by Allah (God) for His special purposes and assignments. My views aside, I do respect the many views that are held with respect the nature of angels. Muslims are required to believe in angels as part of our faith tradition, but a quick survey of Muslims will prove that how we understand what angels are varies. Nevertheless, men and women are possessed of spirit or 'ruh' (Greek: *pneuma*) and so the view of those of us inside the Nation of Islam that angels are human beings who possess and are guided by Allah's divine spirit, may just be the best rapprochement for the major opposing views of the concept of angels; corporeal versus ethereal.

And I think I can speak for all Muslims when I say that I am happy that angels are dispatched by Allah to come to the aid of the believer (smile).

4. Allah delivers the believers from affliction.

Deliverance as a sermon or khutbah subject is more germane to the religion of Christianity than Islam. Yet as we demonstrate in the section of this book that exposes the reader to the Quranic ayats that specify Allah's deliverance of the believers, the idea of divine deliverance of the faithful is a strong theme in the Holy Qur'an. A sample of those verses are as follows:

In the name of Allah, the Beneficent, the Merciful.
10:103 Then **We deliver Our messengers and those who believe** - even so (now); it is binding on Us to deliver the believers.
26:118 So judge Thou between me and them openly, and **deliver me and the believers who are with me.**
27:53 And **We delivered those who believed and kept their duty**.

The Divine Messenger of Allah is the agent of Deliverance. He must deliver the message and deliver the people.

The Messenger is called also the *Apostle* of God. The root of the word *apostle* is the word *post*. *Apostle* means "one who is sent forth." The word *post* is also the root of the word *postal*. *Post* is also connected to military soldiers. One holding a *post* is called a *sentinel*. To be delivered one must be on a route, or path or *trail*. The trail is frequently beset with *trials*. Surah Two of the Maulana Muhammad Ali Translation of the Holy Qur'an includes a section entitled *Hard Trials Are Necessary To Establish Truth*. Many of us describe our past as receiving an education in the *school of hard knocks* or trials. And as this volume attempts to show Quranically and universally hard trials are part and parcel of the process of the believer being *delivered*. Sometimes packages that are *delivered* are bruised and look battered. They often get damaged in the process of deliverance. Deliveries can also be tracked; they can be lost and found, and deliveries can be delayed.

Notice the previous paragraph and all its italicized words. Those italicized words comprise what can be called the vocabulary of deliverance. Each of those words has a dual meaning and purpose. Each of those words are taken from the world of religion and the world of mail delivery. We highlight them because they drive home this very strong theme resident within the religion of Islam of deliverance.

THE VOCABULARY OF DELIVERANCE

Words that make up the strong theme of deliverance as expressed in religion. Each word has a denoted meaning that is included in this listing. But each word also has a spiritual significance and meaning that is found in the scriptures of the Holy Qur'an and in the religious teaching of the world's sacred texts.

The Vocabulary of Deliverance	Dictionary Definition
Apostle	a leader or prominent advocate of a religion or reform movement
Deliver	to send or bring (something) to an intended destination or recipient; to help give birth to; to set free, release, or save; to direct or hurl.
Parcel	a distinct piece of land, often a portion of a larger tract; an essential part of something; a group of people or things having some common characteristic; an object, article, container, or quantity of something wrapped or packed up; small package; bundle.
Post	a position or duty to which one is assigned; a military base; the organized delivery of mail, or an instance of such delivery; by mail or courier; after; later than.
Postal	of or relating to the mail service.
Send	to cause to go; to direct or propel to a certain place or point.
Sent	past tense and past participle of send
Sentinel	one that stands guard or watches; sentry; to keep watch over; guard.
Trail	a path or course across rough territory, through woods, or the like.
Travail	strenuous and often painful or exhausting work; toil; trouble, sorrow, or suffering; anguish; the effort and pain of childbirth.

Travel	to move forward in any way; to pass over or through; the movement of persons and vehicles on a certain route or through a given place.
Trial	in law, an examination of evidence presented to a judicial tribunal, usually in order to determine a person's guilt or innocence; the act or process of testing; a subjection to suffering, pain, or hardship; a person or thing that taxes one's patience.

Why does Allah permit and ordain suffering on the believers?

The Most Honorable Elijah Muhammad said that the most important question is not *who, what, when, where, or how.* He said that the most important question is *why.*

We now examine what we can determine as some of the reasoning behind why Allah permits and ordain suffering for the believers. Our study yields three major reasons.

1. To go from believers to knowers.

As a student of scripture it has often fascinated me that when the Holy Qur'an reports the words of the devil (Shaitan or Iblis) it does so revealing his *knowingness* of the reality of Allah (God). In other words, Shaitan never doubts or wavers over the question of the existence and power of the supreme being. This is fascinating because as believers we are often prone to go through periods where we demonstrate doubt or uncertainty. But Shaitan never doubts.

In fact Holy Qur'an 14:22 records the following commentary from Shaitan (Satan, the devil):

And Satan will say when the matter is decided: "It was Allah Who gave you a promise of Truth: I too promised, but I failed in my promise to you. I had no authority over you except to call you but ye listened to me: then reproach not me, but reproach your own souls. I cannot listen to your cries, nor can ye listen to mine. I reject

your former act in associating me with Allah. For wrong-doers
there must be a grievous penalty."

This passage depicts that even the devil himself is certain of the
Day of Judgment and will disavow any allegiance that man has falsely
given to him. He knows that Allah (God) is the only reality, the only
authority and that it is to Allah that all matters are returned.

What about us? How do we become certain and sure? How do
we go from being believers to knowers?

Belief is considered to be the absence of certainty. The footnote
to Surah 69 Ayat 51 in the Yusuf Ali Translation of the Holy Qur'an
outlines three types of certainty.

Footnote 5673: All Truth is in itself certain. But as received by
men, and understood with reference to men's psychology, certainty
may have certain degrees. There is the probability or certainty
resulting from the application of man's power of judgment and his
appraisement of evidence. This is *'ilm al yaqin*, certainty by
reasoning or inference. Then there is the certainty of seeing
something with our own eyes. "Seeing is believing." This is *'ain al
yaqin*, certainty by personal inspection. See 102:5, 7. Then, as
here, there is the absolute Truth, with no possibility of error of
judgment or error of the eye, (which stands for any instrument of
sense-perception and any ancillary aids, such as microscopes, etc.).
This absolute Truth is the *haqq al yaqin* spoken of here.

Translator Maulana Muhammad Ali similarly describes these
three types of certainty in a footnote to Ayat 8 of Surah 102.

Footnote 8a.: Verses 5 - 8 are considered as disclosing three
degrees of certainty - *'ilm al yaqin*, *'ain al-yaqin* and *haqq al-
yaqin*, i.e., certainty by inference, certainty by sight and certainty
by realization. A man can by inference attain to a certainty of the
existence of hell in this very life (vv. 5 and 6); after his death he
will see hell with his own eyes (v. 7); but a perfect manifestation
of it will be realized by him on the day of Resurrection (v. 8).

g questioned about the boons implies tasting of the
ishment for failing to make right use of what was granted to
. But the words may also be taken as applying to this life. By
dering on the very nature of evil a man can become certain of
this being the certainty by inference. Then he can acquire a
in knowledge by sight, by seeing the fate of others. Lastly, he
ade to realize it by disasters being brought upon himself.

Allah carries the believers through suffering and pain that only
deliver us from. We come to understand this suffering because it
cterized by the fact that no powerful person that we know can
us. No family member that we depend on can relieve our pain.
ney is of no help in our ordeal. When these situations arise it
clear that we can't deliver ourselves. Yet somehow we escape.
w get what we need. Miraculously we are healed and there is no
discernable reason why. It is at this point that the believer knows
or she has been delivered by Allah (God). He delivered us and
d a way out for us as He promised us in His word. It is then that
no longer believers in God, we become knowers of God, for we
et Him in our hour of suffering. The Honorable Minister Louis
an is no longer a believer, he is a knower. He was taken to
door three times and delivered.

Should not Minister Farrakhan's great suffering be a message
llah to us, that as He delivered His Servant, He will also deliver

ring is part of the path to becoming God.

Master Fard Muhammad came to make us into Gods. The
of becoming Gods when were dead Negroes (from the Greek
dead) is the path of the Originator of the heavens and the Earth.
The Original Man went through pain inside triple darkness to
Himself and the universe of light around us.

Minister Farrakhan in his pioneering lecture *Who Is God*, the
pt of which appears in Self-Improvement Study Guide 19, said
Originator:

The Honorable Elijah Muhammad taught us that God had to develop brain in order to think through darkness. It took pain and eons of time for God to build Himself up in the darkness. He was Light of Himself and had Light in Himself. Since the basis of His Life is electricity, He had Light in Himself. From His own Brain, He envisioned Sun and then called it into existence. The Honorable Elijah Muhammad said Allah formed Himself - not from a mother, but out of the dark womb of space. Space and the darkness of it became His womb and He came out of that darkness.

We understand this process because the Honorable Elijah Muhammad said to Minister Farrakhan, "Brother, I want your mind. I want you to line your mind up with my mind so that there be one mind." The Honorable Minister Louis Farrakhan said he later asked Bro. Jabril Muhammad, just how could the Honorable Elijah Muhammad make his mind to line up with his own mind. He said it is easy brother, he just takes you through the same thing he went through.

The Honorable Elijah Muhammad wrote about the suffering that he went through as being the path to becoming one with his teacher Master W. Fard Muhammad. He writes in a section entitled *Persecution Follows The Coming of God* in the book *Message To The Blackman in America*:

He (Mr. W. F. Muhammad, God in person) chose to suffer three and half years to show his love for his people, who have suffered over three hundred years at the hands of a people who by nature are evil and wicked and have no good in them. He was persecuted, sent to jail in 1932, and ordered out of Detroit, on May 26, 1933. He came to Chicago in the same year and was arrested almost immediately on his arrival and placed behind prison bars. He submitted himself with all humbleness to his persecutors. Each time he was arrested, he sent for me so that I might see and learn the price of Truth for us, the so-called American Negroes (members of the Asiatic nation). He was well able to save himself from such suffering, but how else was the scripture to be fulfilled? We followed in his footsteps, suffering the same persecution.

Allah carries the believers on a path of pain and suffering to produce in us His mind. The Holy Qur'an 2:138 states the believers take Allah's coloring and Allah is best at coloring. This *colouring* is an English word but the Arabic root word from which it is translated is *sabagha*. *The Dictionary of the Holy Qur'an* by Abdul Manan Omar provides this meaning for the word *sabagha:*

sabagha

To dye, colour, baptize, dip, immerse, hue, assume the attribute, mode, mature, code of law, religion. **sibghatun**: Dye; Religion; Nature; Attribute; etc. In the Holy Qur'ân (2:138) the attributes of God and His code of law is called God's *Sibghah*. This word has been adopted there as a hint to Christians that the baptism of water does not effect any change in a person. It is *Takhalluq bi Akhlâq Allâh* that is the adoption of God's attributes and broad principle of faith bring about the real change in the mind and character. It is through this "baptism" that the new birth takes place. According to the Arabic usage sometimes when it is intended strongly to induce a person to do a certain thing the verb is omitted, as in 2:138 and only the object is mentioned. Therefore in the translation of that verse one must add such verb as *Khudhû* i.e. assume, or adapt. **Sibghun**: Condiment; Sauce; Relish; Savour.

This concept of God's color being a metaphor for His Attributes and His Nature brings to mind common English idioms or phrases that use color to reflect the nature of a person's mind or thinking. We are familiar with such phrases as: "She is green with envy," or "He is blue with sadness," or "The enemy was red with anger."

A *green* person often describes a naïve person or someone who is in someway a neophyte to a task or group. Cowardice is associated with the color yellow. Strength as well as evil is associated with the color black. While white is used to communicate purity and innocence. I am sure that an interior designer could go into much greater detail about color and what it symbolizes in people as well as inanimate objects. But what we want to understand is that the believer is on a path to become a possessor of the mind and spirit of Allah (God). His attributes should be

imprinted across our personality. The nature of His thinking should be
evidenced in our world-view and how we make decisions so that the
outcomes and results of our lives are in harmony with His divine will.
To achieve this exalted state of existence requires suffering on our part.

3. To produce the forces necessary for God-like creativity

The great Turkish Author Harun Yahya writes in his book *The
Secret Behind Our Trials*:

The Muslim Of Difficult Times

The quality of a Muslim's belief and moral character is revealed in
difficult times. Under such circumstances, we see their superior
morality, courage, patience, trust, perception, fortitude, tolerance,
willingness to forgive, self-sacrifice, mercy, humanity,
appreciation, conscience, and composure. "The Muslim of
difficult times" indicates an individual who endures every
difficulty, frustration, and deprivation while displaying the
qualities listed above. Such people never compromise their moral
character, encounter every eventuality with great maturity and
trust in Allah, see the reason for everything that happens and the
good in it, and exhort others to practice the same superior morality.
As The Qur'an says: "When they came at you from above and
below, when your eyes rolled and your hearts rose to your throats
. . ." (Surah al-Ahzab, 10), these difficult times are when believers
undergo serious testing and are beset by frustrations. When we
speak of difficult times, some examples come to the mind of
people who do not know Allah: a natural disaster, losing a job,
bankruptcy, and similar events. But for those with faith, the
difficult moments (may) refer to more serious situations: a time
when a person is deprived of his or her most basic requirements,
and when the frustrations are far more serious than those
experienced in daily life. The Qur'an defines such times when "the
heart rises to the throat" as periods when every imaginable kind of
difficulty, illness, and disaster falls upon a person one after
another, such as when they are thrown out of their house, driven
from their country, confronted with traps set just for them, as well

as their family and people, and they are subject to spiritual oppression. The Qur'an provides examples of the difficulties experienced by the Prophets and devout believers. As we said earlier, devout believers have been brought through and endured many serious trials, for: Or did you suppose that you would enter the Garden without facing the same as those who came before you? Poverty and illness afflicted them and they were shaken to the point that the Messenger and those who believed with him asked: "When is Allah's help coming?" Be assured that Allah's help is very near. (Surah al-Baqara, 214) In this verse, Allah announces that all people will undergo difficulties and gives the good news that those who are patient will have good things for eternity. In these times, the difference between "Muslims of moments of distress" and "fair-weather Muslims" will become evident. Members of the first group respond to their difficulties and frustrations in this way: Those who, when disaster strikes them, say: "We belong to Allah and to Him we will return." (Surah al-Baqara, 156)

We are believers who come to faith as one world is going out and another world is coming in.   This means that we are believers at the most difficult time in the history of man. Allah hopes to use us to remake the world, to be the builders of a new heaven and a new earth. The Honorable Minister Louis Farrakhan said that the new heaven and the new earth mentioned in the scriptures means a new spiritual, political and economic reality. It means new systems and new institutions, which replace the old systems and institutions of this world that are based on rebellion to Allah (God) and his prescriptive way of life for man.

The prophets of God in both the Bible and the Holy Qur'an have prophesied the end of this word due to that which it gives to the people that Minister Farrakhan calls *license*. *License* is the root word of the word *licentious*. The dictionary definition of the word *licentious* is to be *abandoned, disorderly, dissolute, immoral, impure, lascivious, lax, lewd, libertine, libidinous, lubricious (literary), lustful, profligate, promiscuous, sensual, uncontrollable, uncontrolled, uncurbed, unruly, wanton.* This definition is a fitting description of the human condition and calls to mind that which the Bible records as part of Paul's letter to Timothy, which we cited earlier.

The license that the people of the world take to rebel and disregard divine commands and instructions actually is the opposite of freedom, because licentious behaviors frequently lead to crime and the disruption of society. So the licentious person who is caught performing criminal acts in the name of his so-called freedom is soon arrested and loses the freedom he or she thought they were exercising. The idea and concept of freedom is synonymous with behaviors and conduct that support peace and order in the society. The free person is *chaste, law-abiding, lawful, moral, principled, proper, scrupulous, and virtuous.* For such behaviors there is no prohibition against. This is why we are taught that our righteousness will sustain us.

The divine destruction of this world is important for us as believers to remember. It lays emphasis on our own troubles and trials. It helps to put it into perspective. It also helps to communicate the need for an enlightened view of suffering, one that depicts suffering as the seed-bed of the force of creativity.

Cedric Muhammad writes in his very excellent book series *The Entrepreneurial Secret* on the subject *The Secret of Suffering* that:

Pain and suffering produces a spiritual process within the individual. The spiritual process within the individual is the basis of entrepreneurial activity, which is the foundation of business activity, which is the basis of economic activity. Therefore there can't be a real separation between economics and spirituality.

By spirituality we mean the deeper hidden or unseen animating reality or intention that exists behind, beyond, or underneath an act, appearance, or superficial reality. There is often a deeper, hidden or unseen process or chain or events that gives birth or delivery to a business, product or service.

When we study the life of great men and women, we see the value of suffering in creating that which gives benefit to others and ourselves.

that you can think of that is admirable in any field or profession ved at such a destination as the product of great suffering.

In studying just how to turn suffering into creative muse, the of Musa in the Holy Qur'an is instructive (Surah 18: 60-82). was at the junction of two rivers and he and his companion the loss of their sustenance - a fish. Musa and his companion led past the point of the junction of the two rivers, but when it to eat they determined that they would return to the junction of rivers; the place where the companion had revealed that they had r fish.

It was when they returned to the journey of the two rivers, the their loss, when they found the wise man Khidr, who would Musa to be the beneficiary of special knowledge and wisdom, that has been described as mystical insight. We glean from this a valuable lesson and an apt illustration. We learn that this of two rivers represents the confluence of forces that lead to the forces that ultimately give meaning and purpose to our g. The junction of the two rivers is an excellent symbol of how life we find ourselves at the intersection of loss and reward.

So the difficulty factor attached to being a Muslim at the end of world and the beginning of Allah's world coupled with the ty we face in seeking to prosper and fulfill our goals in life are all tory. When we in our lives come to places of suffering, we must ledge that the opportunity to suffer is simultaneously an nity for great creativity, happiness, fulfillment and prosperity. If properly our suffering can expose to us the junction or tion where there is the confluence of three powerful forces. An y to remember them is to remember the 3S's:

Suffering: The force of that which our suffering has prepared us for,

Service: The force arising out of our need to be of service to others and

Self: The force of our own desire for success in life-fulfillment.

This intersection of the 3-S's forces us to go through the process of examining ourselves to see what has our suffering and pain has uniquely prepared us to do; how can others benefit by what we have learned and been prepared to do via our suffering; what is the means by which we can serve others and derive a livelihood or income at the same time is where we achieve success in life, supreme happiness, self-actualization, fulfillment. This is the place where our suffering finds its greatest purpose. This sweet spot or strike zone, if you will, is where personal suffering, community service and self service meet. It is a special and necessary alignment that brings harmony and real peace.

The challenge now is for us all to reevaluate our suffering. Become a revisionist historian of your own past. Ask yourself the question: what has my suffering prepared me to offer to others that will also answer my own need for success. I believe that if we use this formula, we will have taken Allah (God's) view of suffering and we will find our purpose and we will find our joy.

As Salaam Alaikum.

NURSE FROM THE HOLY QUR'AN

Man and Woman's Destined Embodiment Of
Allah's Divine Word

The title of this book comes from guidance and counsel given by the Most Honorable Elijah Muhammad to his top student the Honorable Minister Louis Farrakhan. He said to the Minister, "Brother when you get into trouble, nurse from your Holy Qur'an."

The English word "nurse," when used as a verb, is defined by the dictionary as meaning:

> to nourish at the breast, to suckle; to take nourishment from the breast of; to rear or educate; to promote the development or progress of; to manage with care or economy (Example sentence: He nursed the business through hard times); to take charge of and watch over; to care for and wait on (as a sick person); to attempt to cure by care and treatment; to hold in one's memory or consideration (Example sentence: She nursed a grievance); to use, handle, or operate carefully so as to conserve energy or avoid injury or pain (Example sentence: He must nurse his sprained ankle); to consume slowly or over a long period (Example phrase: nurse a cup of coffee)

The etymology of the word "nurse" shows that it shares a Latin root with the words *nourish* and *nutritious*. Its morphology reveals that the Arabic word *Nur* makes up the first 3 letters of the word. Surah 24 of the Holy Qur'an is entitled *al-Nur* that is translated as meaning *the Light*. Al-Nur is one of the names or attributes of Allah and the Holy Qur'an.

The Bible and the Holy Qur'an are filled with references to the contrasting concepts of light and darkness. These concepts are often used to symbolize states of the human condition. To be *in the light* or *walking in the light (Holy Qur'an 57:28; Isaiah 2:5, 9:2,42:16)* is to be enlightened, but not necessarily in the classical sense of how the term *enlightenment* is used.

The light of scripture is God Himself and His Anointed Messenger(s) is (are) the lens through which the people are able to see that light *(Holy Qur'an 91:1, 33:46, 36:13-14, John 8:12)*. The word of Allah (God) is what remains after the prophets and messengers are no longer present among the people. The word therefore becomes the primary means through which believers relate to Allah (God). To prove this we cite the words of The Honorable Elijah Muhammad who said "When you want to talk to Allah (God), read the Holy Qur'an." The Islamic prayer service (salaat), which is the prescribed way of communicating with Allah, is yet made up of the words of Allah (God) found in the Holy Qur'an. So even in prayer we takeaway that Allah's word is powerful and the primary means through which we relate to Him.

On a higher level we can also understand that the real destiny of the believer is to become an embodiment of the ideas, principles, concepts, and truths contained in the word of Allah. Islam teaches that man is to become Allah's *khalifah* or vice-gerent. And even though throughout man's long history of deviation from the path and principles of Allah (God), the primary response from Allah is to offer to the people a man and a book; a prophet and a prophecy; a messenger and a message; a reminder and a revealed word. This suggests that man and woman can only make a return to the exalted state from which we fell by means of internalizing the message contained in the books or word of Allah (God). And this understanding is consistent with the creation narrative that we find in the Holy Qur'an. In this narrative Adam is prepared for the role of *khalifah* by receiving a special education. The Holy Qur'an says that Allah taught Adam "all the names." Translator Maulana Muhammad Ali includes in his footnote to Surah 2 Ayat 31:

"He taught him the attributes of things and their descriptions and their characteristics, for the attributes of a thing are indicative of its nature"

So the special education of Adam was preparatory in order for him to serve Allah as the vice-gerent of Allah. This reinforces our premise of that special word, instruction, education, message or teaching is part and parcel to the human being achieving the original aim and purpose for existence - to be Allah's *khalifah*. The Dictionary of the Holy Qur'an defines the word *khalifah* as:

khalifah

Supreme chief; Successor; Religious head. Ibn Masûd and Ibn 'Abbas explain this word as one who judges among or rules the creatures of God by his command. The word Khalifah in 2:30 refers also to the children of Adam, i.e., the whole of mankind, the correctness of their view is corroborated by the Holy Qur'an itself (6:165).

But the concept of man as Allah's khalifah also reinforces the other aspect of our premise. Since the angels are not polytheistic and they were commanded by Allah to make obeisance or to bow in submission to Adam (Holy Qur'an 2:34, 7:11,17:61, 18:50, 20:116) what

 had Allah made of Adam? He had made Adam a God. He had conferred upon Adam an authority, a knowledge, a form (sura: body) and an indwelling spirit; all coming from Himself. In the Nation of Islam, we are taught that Master Fard Muhammad is the "words of the Holy Qur'an clothed in flesh." This description of Him is the essence of the idea of divine embodiment that is connected to the concept of *khalifah.* Master Fard Muhammad embodies the ideas, concepts, principles and power of Allah (God) that is articulated within the pages of the Holy Qur'an. He demonstrates that the book and the man are one. Another way of looking at it would be to say that since the book came through man, specifically the Holy Prophet Muhammad ibn Abdullah (saw), the book's ultimate destination is to live within man and woman. From the Christian or Biblical perspective, we could cite the Book of John, chapter 1 that says *the "word became flesh and dwelled among men"* to further plumb the depth of this idea.

Again, the idea of embodiment or incarnation is a strong theme within the Holy Qur'an and Bible. The believer in Allah must ultimately embody the word of Allah - Holy Qur'an. This is the aim of the submission part of the definition of the word Muslim *as one who submits entirely to the will of Allah (God).* We can't know the will and can't submit to His Will unless we immerse ourselves in the study of the Holy Qur'an. And since whatever we submit to is what we ultimately become

one with, our submission to the will of Allah produces oneness with Him and His Creation. It produces the real tangible outcome that we all desire which is to be in harmony with the universe so that we may extract from it that which satisfies our needs, wants and righteous desires.

That man is to be the embodiment of Allah's Divine Book is perhaps the reason why when we study the anatomy of a book we find its nomenclature taken from the anatomy of man. A book has an area on it called a head band; it has a spine; books wear book jackets; folding down the top edges of the book's pages is called making ears on the book; the bottom of the book is a place for footnotes; book pages have headers and footers; and the central theme of the book's contents is called the heart of the book.

This book the Holy Qur'an is unique. The Most Honorable Elijah Muhammad said, "The Holy Qur'an is the greatest book there is. It is a unique book." So we want to nurse from it in order to become one with Allah (God). We want to nurse from it to walk in His Light, which is His Wisdom that raises us from the darkness of ignorance and a life based on ignorance. We want to nurse from it to care for, cure and heal ourselves and the people of this world.

The Believer As Pupil

I referred to the Honorable Minister Louis Farrakhan as the *top student* of the Most Honorable Elijah Muhammad. The title of *student* deserves some exploring because it is very rich in meaning and symbolism.

The Collins Dictionary of English states that the word *student* is "etymologically derived through Middle English from the Latin second-type conjugation verb *studere*, meaning "to direct one's zeal at"; hence a *student* could be described as "one who directs zeal at a subject." In its widest use, student is used for anyone who is learning.

The word student and the word pupil are synonyms for one
[...]. The word pupil is defined as "apprentice, novice, pupil, disciple,
[...] student, a person who is studying, usually in a school." A pupil
[...] under the close supervision of a teacher, either because of youth
[...] specialization in some branch of study: {Example phrases: *a grade-
[...] pupil; the pupil of a famous musician}*. A disciple is one who
[...] the teachings or doctrines of a person whom he or she considers
[...] a master or authority: {Example phrases: *a disciple of
[...]borg}*. Scholar, once meaning the same as pupil, is today usually
[...] to one who has acquired wide erudition in some field of learning:
[...]ple Phrase: *a great Latin scholar}*. A student is a person attending
[...]ational institution or someone who has devoted much attention
[...]ticular problem: {Example Phrases: *a college student; a student
[...]ics}*.

The idea that a student is also a pupil lends itself to our
[...]hing subject of Nursing from the Holy Qur'an. Above we
[...]ledged the Holy Qur'an as a book of divine light or wisdom. We
[...] how the *nur* in the word *nurse* is the same as the *al-Nur* that is
[...]y Qur'an and Allah (God) Himself. When we study the Holy
[...] we are being exposed to and are absorbing the divine Light of
[...] As students of the Holy Qur'an we are also manifesting and
[...]strating the meaning of a *pupil* where it is described as being a
[...] human anatomy.

Webster's defines pupil as "the expanding and contracting
[...] in the iris of the eye, through which light passes to the retina."
[...]pedia Britannica notes "in the anatomy of the eye, the opening
[...] the iris through which light passes before reaching the lens and
[...] ocused onto the retina. The size of the opening is governed by the
[...] of the iris, which rapidly constrict the pupil when exposed to
[...] light and expand (dilate) the pupil in dim light. Parasympathetic
[...] fibers from the third (oculomotor) cranial nerve innervate the
[...] that causes constriction of the pupil, whereas sympathetic nerve
[...] control dilation. The pupillary aperture also narrows when
[...]ng on close objects and dilates for more distant viewing. At its
[...]m contraction, the adult pupil may be less than 1 mm (0.04 inch)
[...]eter, and it may increase up to 10 times to its maximum diameter.

The size of the human pupil may also vary as a result of age, disease, trauma, or other abnormalities within the visual system, including dysfunction of the pathways controlling pupillary movement. Thus, careful evaluation of the pupils is an important part of both eye and neurologic exams.

The pupil of the eye expands and contracts based on light intensity. We as pupils or students of the Light (*Nur*) of Allah (God) must be subject to and in submission to the divine Light of Allah's Word. The bright light that makes the eye's pupil constrict is analogous to the Restrictive Law of Islam that restricts the believer to the behaviors that are in alignment with the Will of Allah. The dim light that expands the pupil is analogous to the poorly lit landscape of human topography that is the American people. Muslims are to be a light and have a light that enables the people to see clearly the right path as distinguished from the path of error.

57:28 O you who believe, keep your duty to Allah and believe in His Messenger — He will give you two portions of His mercy, and **give you a light in which you shall walk**, and forgive you. And Allah is Forgiving, Merciful —

There are other verses within the English Translation of the Holy Qur'an that describe Allah as expanding the breast of the believer. Consider the following ayats:

6:125 So whomsoever Allah intends to guide, He **expands his breast** for Islam,

20:25 He said: My Lord, **expand my breast** for me:

94:1 Have We not **expanded for thee thy breast**,

Only Allah (God) knows the true interpretation of His Word but as believers we are permitted to think, study, reflect and meditate over His Word to extract guiding spiritual principles to benefit ourselves and the people we are to serve. So based upon the definition of the anatomical pupil and how light expands and contracts it, we see that the spiritual pupil - the believer - is destined to be developed, cultivated, governed and preserved as a result of their submission to the Light contained in the Word of Allah (God). And nursing, or intensely studying the Holy Qur'an, is the exercise we must engage in routinely in order to be exposed to the Light.

The Honorable Minister Louis Farrakhan's abilities are therefore our example of what we will be able to do once we make nursing from the Holy Qur'an a habit. Minister Farrakhan's integrity is an example of how principled we can be when we integrate nursing from the Holy Qur'an into our daily activities. Minister Farrakhan's love is an example of the love we will be able to give as well as receive when we dive into the mighty and luminous Word of Allah (God). He is among us a man that is baptized in that Word and we can say that when we are in his presence we feel the Spirit of Allah (God) that the Word of Allah (God) produces.

I hope that we will embrace the study of the Holy Qur'an and the study of the Honorable Minister Louis Farrakhan so that we can fulfill the purpose for which we have been brought forth from the wombs of our mothers. And that is to share time and space with one who forever changes the course of the history of humanity while at the same time serving that one who is literally Allah's (God's) instrument of universal change.

The Healing Milk of The Holy Qur'an

One of the great virtues that the Muslim is instructed to possess is to remain in all that we do God-Conscious. The word *taqwa* is the Arabic word used for this state of being enjoined of the believers. Nursing from the Holy Qur'an enables us to remain *taqwa* unlike anything else. When a baby nurses from his mother's breast, he spends a lot of time with the breast because he understands that from the breast comes the milk that nourishes him and satisfies the discomfort of hunger. So the idea of familiarity is a part of nursing from the Holy Qur'an; we must spend time with the book so that just as the baby is familiar with the mother's breast in an intimate way, we become intimately acquainted with Allah's Word. What babies get from breast milk that amazes scientists is materially what the believer can get from the Holy Qur'an in a mental, emotional and spiritual way.

The website *Ask Dr. Sears* published an article entitled *How Human Milk Protects Babies From Illness.* The following is an excerpt:
How Human Milk Protects Babies From Illness

Human milk is more than food. It's a complex living substance, like blood, with a long list of active germ-fighting and health-promoting ingredients. These help protect babies against all kinds of infections, common and not-so-common.

A drop of breast milk contains around one million white blood cells. These cells, called macrophages ("big eaters"), gobble up germs. Breast milk is also power-packed with immunoglobulin A (IgA), which coats the lining of babies' immature intestines, preventing germs from leaking through. Secretory IgA also works to prevent food allergies. By coating the intestinal lining like a protective paint, it prevents molecules of foreign foods from getting into the bloodstream to set up an allergic reaction.

Colostrum, the milk mothers produce in the first few days after birth, is especially rich in IgA, just at the time when the newborn is first exposed to the outside world and needs protection from germs and foreign substances entering his body. Colostrum also contains higher amounts of white blood cells and infection-fighting substances than mature milk. Think of colostrum as your baby's first important immunization.

As babies grow, mother's milk continues to provide important protection against infection and disease. Human infants receive antibodies through the placenta, but these are gradually used up during the first six months. Human milk fills in the immunity gap until baby's own immune system matures and kicks in. Even babies that continue to nurse into toddlerhood benefit from the many immune factors in their mother's milk.

Immunities made-to-order. Each mother provides custom-designed milk to protect her infant. When a baby is exposed to a new germ, mother's body manufactures antibodies to that germ. These antibodies show up in her milk and are passed along to her baby. Many a nursing mother can tell the story of the entire family - dad, mom, siblings - coming down with the flu and the nursing baby having the mildest case, or not getting sick at all. When mother comes down with a bug, the best thing she can do for her baby is to keep breastfeeding.

Breastfed Babies are Healthier

Derrick and Patrice Jelliffe, pioneers in breastfeeding research, stated that breastfed infants are "biochemically different." This difference in body chemistry may be the reason they are healthier. While babies are breastfeeding, they have fewer and less serious respiratory infections, less diarrhea, and less vomiting. When breastfed babies do become ill, they are less likely to become dehydrated and need hospitalization.

Here are some specific ways in which breastfeeding protects babies from illness:

Friendly to little ears. Ear infections are a childhood nuisance, often following on the heels of stuffy noses and colds. The middle ear fills with fluid, and eventually that fluid becomes infected, causing pain, especially in the middle of the night. Repeated ear infections, or those that go untreated, can lead to hearing loss. This is an important concern in young children, since hearing difficulties can interfere with language, and language problems can later affect reading skills.

Breastfeeding protects against ear infections in four possible ways:

The many germ-fighting ingredients in human milk keep harmful bacteria from bothering baby, so that stuffed-up noses and ears are less likely to become infected middle ears.

Because breastfed babies are fed in a more upright position, they're less likely to experience milk backing up through the eustachian tube into their ears; if this does happen during a breastfeeding session, human milk is less irritating to the tissues of the middle ear than infant formula.

Breastfed babies have fewer, or at least less severe, colds than formula-fed babies. Fewer colds mean fewer ear infections.

Breastfed babies have fewer respiratory allergies, another cause of fluid building up in the middle ear, which sets the stage for bacteria to grow.

Protects tiny tummies. Human milk excels at protecting babies from diarrhea and tummy upsets. This is important not only for individual babies but also on a global scale. Diarrhea is a leading cause of infant mortality worldwide, and breastfeeding is the simplest, most cost- effective way to protect babies from repeated bouts of gastrointestinal illness.

Another way in which breastfeeding protects tiny tummies is by promoting the growth of healthful bacteria in the intestines. Intestines are healthiest when you can keep the right "bugs" in the bowels. The healthful bacteria, known as bifidus bacteria, do good things for the body in return for a warm place to live. They manufacture vitamins and nutrients and keep the harmful bacteria in check. The high levels of lactose in breast milk particularly encourage the growth of the healthful resident bacteria Lactobacillus bifidus.
Protects against other infection. Studies have found that breastfeeding protects against a wide variety of other diseases. Here's a partial list: Haemophilus influenza type B; Pneumonia caused by Streptococcus pneumonia; Meningitis; Infant botulism; Urinary tract infections; Cholera; Salmonella; E. coli infections; Respiratory syncytial virus.

There are also studies that report that breast milk contains
properties that improve the intelligence of babies. But we can see just
how important breast milk is for its immunization properties, and how it
really supports growth, hearing and digestion. Surah 9 of the Holy
Qur'an in the Muhammad Ali translation is entitled *The Immunity*. The
Qur'an is also known as *al-Shifa, The Healing*. These titles indicate
the spiritual, emotional and mental medicinal properties of Allah's
Word. We are to take away from such descriptions of the Holy Qur'an
that there is medicine in it for us and for this sin-sick world. The
conditions listed in the citation above are physical ailments that breast
milk fights. The 19 spiritual diseases identified in Paul's letter to
Timothy (2Timothy Chapter 3) are mental and spiritual ailments that
milk in general and specifically the Holy Qur'an fights.

Lastly, is a recommendation for an excellent exercise. It is
borrowed from the world of sports. When neophyte quarterbacks get
set for their leadership role on their respective teams, many of them
want to master the play book. So they take note cards and affix them
to the visible sleeve on their forearms to serve as a guide throughout the
game. This training wheel approach does not have to be confined to the
sports world. It is a great tool for helping neophyte Muslims nurse and
grow strong from the Holy Qur'an (and long-time Muslims as well). So
go to the scripture section of this book and perhaps you will find some
verses that quickly become your favorite. Or open your Holy Qur'an
up to your favorite verses. Write them down on a card and keep it
with you in your purse, backpack or wallet. Read them daily for the
purpose of memorizing them. And don't just memorize what the verses
actually say, memorize where they are located-chapter (surah) and verse.
You will find that you will soon have a running catalogue of ayats
in your memory bank from which you can always make a withdrawal
in times of difficulty in your life.

May Allah bless us all to fall in love with His Word and feed
from it often so that we become one with Him and one with one another.

SCRIPTURE

ALLAH

Refuge in Allah is the ultimate solace for the believers. We are taught to seek refuge in Him, but oft-times, even though we believe in Him, we don't know too much about Allah. So it becomes difficult to seek refuge in Him whom we are ignorant of. He gave us a book so that we may learn of Him and His Attributes and His Methodology or Way. His book contains a prescription for how life should be lived in order to be in harmony with Allah (God) and His creation. And when it is said to seek refuge in Allah, what is specifically meant is this prescriptive way of life that we are to find safety, security and success in. This section is devoted to ayats or verses that communicate the way in which Allah relates to creation and to those who believe in Him. Muslims are taught to strive to remain *Taqwa* or God conscious. This section is devoted to facilitating more than just a consciousness of Allah (God's) existence but to also establish within the mind of the believers a catalog of specific Qur'anic verses that can instantly be recalled when difficult situations arise. Knowing the methodology or way of Allah (God) prevents unnecessary panic during any apparent crises and also generates a healthy sense of urgency when the situation deems it necessary, both based on our familiarity with how Allah (God) has described Himself on the pages of the Holy Qur'an. Remember that those who need refuge are those that are in danger or are in harm's way. And as long as we are not living the prescriptive life specified in the Holy Qur'an we are indeed in great danger. We are specifically in danger if we are not living according to the nature in which we have been created and not living according to the divine purpose for which Allah created man and woman. Thusly, our non-compliance with, rebellion to, and resistance to Allah's will cause us to nullify our existence. We are, in this rebellious state, less than the rest of creation. Allah's creation, earth, plant and animal life are all put into the service of man. Yet all of creation lives according to the nature in which it is created and therefore justifies its remaining in existence. It is only the human being who is frequently unwilling to submit, which means to live in harmony with Allah (God) and His Creation. And this misuse of free will, better known as rebellion, produces stress and inordinate suffering.

Allah Accepts Repentance

Who forgiveth sin, accepteth repentance, is strict in punishment, and hath a long reach (in all things). There is no god but He: to Him is the final goal. (40:3)

He is the One that accepts repentance from His Servants and forgives sins: and He knows all that ye do. (42:25)

All Good Is From Him

Whatever good, (O man!) happens to thee, is from Allah; but whatever evil happens to thee, is from thy (own) soul. And We have sent thee as a messenger to (instruct) mankind. And enough is Allah for a witness. (4:79)

And it is said to those who guard against evil: What has your Lord revealed? They say, Good. For those who do good in this world is good. And certainly the abode of the Hereafter is better. And excellent indeed is the abode of those who keep their duty. (16:30)

And whatever good you have, it is from Allah; then, when evil afflicts you, to Him do you cry for aid. (16:53)

Allah Brings To Light What Is Hidden

So that they worship not Allah, Who brings forth what is hidden in the heavens and the earth and knows what you hide and what you proclaim. (27:25)

O my son, even if it be the weight of a grain of mustard-seed, even though it be in a rock, or in the heaven or in the earth, Allah will bring it forth. Surely Allah is Knower of subtleties, Aware. (31:16)

Calls To Account

To Allah belongeth all that is in the heavens and on earth. Whether ye show what is in your minds or conceal it, Allah Calleth you to account for it. He forgiveth whom He pleaseth, and punisheth whom He pleaseth, for Allah hath power over all things. (2:284)

Whether We shall show thee (within thy life-time) part of what we promised them or take to ourselves thy soul (before it is all accomplished), thy duty is to make (the Message) reach them: it is our part to call them to account.

See they not that We gradually reduce the land (in their control) from its outlying borders? (Where) Allah commands, there is none to put back His Command: and He is swift in calling to account. (13:40-41)

Therefore, by the Lord, We will, of a surety, call them to account. (15:92)

Or that He may not call them to account in the midst of their goings to and fro, without a chance of their frustrating Him? Or that He may not call them to account by a process of slow wastage - for thy Lord is indeed full of kindness and mercy. (16:46-47)

And they (even) assign, to things they do not know, a portion out of that which We have bestowed for their sustenance! By Allah, ye shall certainly be called to account for your false inventions. (16:56)

If Allah so willed, He could make you all one people: But He leaves straying whom He pleases, and He guides whom He pleases: but ye shall certainly be called to account for all your actions. (16:93)

He does take an account of them (all), and hath numbered them (all) exactly. (19:94)

We shall set up scales of justice for the Day of Judgment, so that not a soul will be dealt with unjustly in the least, and if there be (no more than) the weight of a mustard seed, We will bring it (to account): and enough are We to take account. (21:47)

(It is the practice of those) who preach the Messages of Allah, and fear Him, and fear none but Allah. And enough is Allah to call (men) to account. (33:39)

Have they not travelled in the land and seen what was the end of those who were before them? Mightier than these were they in strength and in fortifications in the land, but Allah destroyed them for their sins. And they had none to protect them from Allah. That was because there came to them their messengers with clear arguments, but they disbelieved, so Allah destroyed them. Surely He is Strong, Severe in Retribution. (40:21-22)

And how many a town which rebelled against the commandment of its Lord and His messengers, so We called it to severe account and We chastised it with a stern chastisement! (65:8)

Then it will be for Us to call them to account. (88:26)

Allah Comes In Between A Man And His Heart

O you who believe, respond to Allah and His Messenger, when he calls you to that which gives you life. And know that Allah comes in between a man and his heart, and that to Him you will be gathered. (8:24)

Allah Created Things In Due Proportions and Truth (for just ends)

It is He who created the heavens and the earth in true (proportions): the day He saith, "Be," behold! It is. His word is the truth. His will be the on the day the trumpet will be blown. He knoweth the unseen as that which is open. For He is the Wise, well acquainted (with all (6:73)

ou not that Allah created the heavens and the earth in Truth? If will, He can remove you and put (in your place) a new creation?

I have fashioned him (in due proportion) and breathed into him pirit, fall ye down in obeisance unto him." (15:29)

created not the heavens and the earth and what is between them truth. And the Hour is surely coming, so turn away with kindly ness. (15:85)

ted the heavens and the earth with truth. Highly exalted be He what they associate (with Him)! (16:3)

ose is the kingdom of the heavens and the earth, and Who did not Himself a son, and Who has no associate in the kingdom, and ated everything, then ordained for it a measure. (25:2)

reated the heavens and the earth with truth. Surely there is a sign or the believers. (29:44)

not reflect within themselves? Allah did not create the heavens earth and what is between them but with truth, and (for) an ed term. And surely most of the people are deniers of the meeting ir Lord. (30:8)

fashioned him in due proportion, and breathed into him ing of His spirit. And He gave you (the faculties of) hearing and d feeling (and understanding): little thanks do ye give! (32:9)

created the heavens and the earth with truth; He makes the night he day and makes the day overtake the night, and He has made and the moon subservient; each one moves on to an assigned ow surely He is the Mighty, the Forgiver. (39:5)

And We did not create the heavens and the earth and that which is between them in sport. We created them but with truth, but most of them know not. (44:38-39)

Allah created the heavens and the earth for just ends, and in order that each soul may find the recompense of what it has earned, and none of them be wronged. (45:22)

We created not the heavens and the earth and all between them but for just ends, and for a Term Appointed: But those who reject Faith turn away from that whereof they are warned. (46:3)

Verily, all things have We created in proportion and measure. (54:49)

He has created the heavens and the earth in just proportions, and has given you shape, and made your shapes beautiful: and to Him is the final Goal. (64:3)

Him Who created thee. Fashioned thee in due proportion, and gave thee a just bias; (82:7)

Who hath created, and further, given order and proportion; (87:2)

By the Soul, and the proportion and order given to it; (91:7)

Allah Encompasses All Things

But to Allah belong all things in the heavens and on earth: And He it is that Encompasseth all things. (4:126)

And when We said to thee: Surely thy Lord encompasses men. And We made not the vision which We showed thee but a trial for men, as also the tree cursed in the Qur'an. And We warn them, but it only adds to their great inordinacy. (17:60)

Those who bear the Throne of Power and those around it celebrate the praise of their Lord and believe in Him and ask protection for those who believe: Our Lord, Thou embracest all things in mercy and knowledge, so protect those who turn (to Thee) and follow Thy way, and save them from the chastisement of hell. (40:7)

Ah indeed! Are they in doubt concerning the Meeting with their Lord? Ah indeed! It is He that doth encompass all things! (41:54)

Allah is He who created seven heavens, and of the earth the like thereof. The command descends among them, that you may know that Allah is Possessor of power over all things, and that Allah encompasses all things in (His) knowledge. (65:12)

Enlarges Provisions and Restricts

Who is it that will offer to Allah a goodly gift, so He multiplies it to him manifold? And Allah receives and amplifies, and to Him you shall be returned. (2:245)

Allah amplifies and straitens provision for whom He pleases. And they rejoice in this world's life. And this world's life, compared with the Hereafter, is only a temporary enjoyment. (13:26)

Verily thy Lord doth provide sustenance in abundance for whom He pleaseth, and He provideth in a just measure. For He doth know and regard all His servants. (17:30)

And those who had envied his position the day before began to say on the morrow: "Ah! It is indeed Allah Who enlarges the provision or restricts it, to any of His servants He pleases! Had it not been that Allah was gracious to us, He could have caused the earth to swallow us up! Ah! Those who reject Allah will assuredly never prosper." (28:82)

Allah makes abundant the means of subsistence for whom He pleases of His servants, or straitens (them) for him. Surely Allah is Knower of all things. (29:62)

See they not that Allah enlarges the provision and restricts it, to whomsoever He pleases? Verily in that are Signs for those who believe. (30:37)

Say: Surely my Lord amplifies and straitens provision for whom He pleases, but most men know not. (34:36)

Say: Surely my Lord amplifies provision for whom He pleases of His servants and straitens (it) for him. And whatsoever you spend, He increases it in reward, and He is the Best of Providers. (34:39)

Know they not that Allah enlarges the provision or restricts it, for any He pleases? Verily, in this are Signs for those who believe! (39:52)

His are the treasures of the heavens and the earth - He amplifies and straitens subsistence for whom He pleases. Surely He is Knower of all things. (42:12)

If Allah were to enlarge the provision for His Servants, they would indeed transgress beyond all bounds through the earth; but he sends (it) down in due measure as He pleases. For He is with His Servants Well-acquainted, Watchful. (42:27)

Now, as for man, when his Lord trieth him, giving him honour and gifts, then saith he, (puffed up), "My Lord hath honoured me." But when He trieth him, restricting his subsistence for him, then saith he (in despair), "My Lord hath humiliated me!" (89:15-16)

For All Things He Has Appointed A Due Proportion

Allah doth know what every female (womb) doth bear, by how much the wombs fall short (of their time or number) or do exceed. Every single thing is before His sight, in (due) proportion. (13:8)

Verily thy Lord doth provide sustenance in abundance for whom He pleaseth, and He provideth in a just measure. For He doth know and regard all His servants. (17:30)

And He provides for him from (sources) he never could imagine. And if any one puts his trust in Allah, sufficient is (Allah) for him. For Allah will surely accomplish his purpose: verily, for all things has Allah appointed a due proportion. (65:3)

Allah Gives Life To The Dead

That it is He Who granteth Laughter and Tears; (2:28)

Didst thou not Turn by vision to those who abandoned their homes, though they were thousands (In number), for fear of death? Allah said to them: "Die." Then He restored them to life. For Allah is full of bounty to mankind, but Most of them are ungrateful. (2:243)

Or like him who passed by a town, and it had fallen in upon its roofs. He said: When will Allah give it life after its death? So Allah caused him to die for a hundred years, then raised him. He said: How long hast thou tarried? He said: I have tarried a day, or part of a day. He said: Nay, thou has tarried a hundred years; but look at thy food and drink -- years have not passed over it! And look at thy ass! And that We may make thee a sign to men. And look at the bones, how We set them together then clothe them with flesh. So when it became clear to him, he said: I know that Allah is Possessor of power over all things. And when Abraham said, My Lord, show me how Thou givest life to the dead, He said: Dost thou not believe? He said: Yes, but that my heart may be at ease. He said: Then take four birds, then tame them to incline to thee, then place on every mountain a part of them, then class them, they will come to thee flying; and know that Allah is Mighty, Wise. (2:259-260)

"Thou causest the night to gain on the day, and thou causest the day to gain on the night; Thou bringest the Living out of the dead, and Thou bringest the dead out of the Living; and Thou givest sustenance to whom Thou pleasest, without measure." (3:27)

Those who listen (in truth), be sure, will accept: as to the dead, Allah will raise them up; then will they be turned unto Him. (6:36)

It is He Who sendeth the winds like heralds of glad tidings, going before His mercy: when they have carried the heavy-laden clouds, We drive them to a land that is dead, make rain to descend thereon, and produce every kind of harvest therewith: thus shall We raise up the dead: perchance ye may remember. (7:57)

Say: Who gives you sustenance from the heaven and the earth, or who controls the hearing and the sight, and who brings forth the living from the dead, and brings for the dead from the living? And who regulates the affair? They will say: Allah. Say then: Will you not then guard against evil? (10:31)

This is so, because Allah is the Reality: it is He Who gives life to the dead, and it is He Who has power over all things. (22:6)

It is He Who brings out the living from the dead, and brings out the dead from the living, and Who gives life to the earth after it is dead: and thus shall ye be brought out (from the dead). (30:19)

It is Allah Who has created you: further, He has provided for your sustenance; then He will cause you to die; and again He will give you life. Are there any of your (false) "Partners" who can do any single one of these things? Glory to Him! And high is He above the partners they attribute (to him)! (30:40)

Then contemplate (O man!) the memorials of Allah's Mercy! How He gives life to the earth after its death: verily the same will give life to the men who are dead: for He has power over all things. (30:50)

Verily We shall give life to the dead, and We record that which they send before and that which they leave behind, and of all things have We taken account in a clear Book (of evidence). (36:12)

Say, "He will give them life Who created them for the first time! For He is Well-versed in every kind of creation! (36:79)

And of His signs is this, that thou seest the earth still, but when We send down water thereon, it stirs and swells. He Who gives it life is surely the Giver of life to the dead. Surely He is Possessor of Power over all things. (41:39)

Or have they taken protectors besides Him? But Allah is the Protector, and He gives life to the dead, and He is Possessor of power over all things. (42:9)

... y not that Allah, Who created the heavens and the earth, and never
... with their creation, is able to give life to the dead? Yea, verily
... power over all things. (46:33)

... enance for (Allah's) Servants; and We give (new) life therewith
... that is dead: Thus will be the Resurrection. (50:11)

... He, (the same), the power to give life to the dead? (75:40)

... when it is His Will, He will raise him up (again). (80:22)

... (Allah) is able to bring him back (to life)! (86:8)

Gives Sustenance

... e gave you the shade of clouds and sent down to you Manna and
... saying: "Eat of the good things We have provided for you" (but
... belled); to us they did no harm, but they harmed their own souls.

... member Abraham said: "My Lord, make this a City of Peace, and
... people with fruits,-such of them as believe in Allah and the Last
... e said: "(Yea), and such as reject Faith, for a while will I grant
... eir pleasure, but will soon drive them to the torment of Fire, an
... tination (indeed)!" (2:126)

... of this world is alluring to those who reject faith, and they scoff
... who believe. But the righteous will be above them on the Day
... rrection; for Allah bestows His abundance without measure on
... He will. (2:212)

... raciously did her Lord accept her: He made her grow in purity
... uty: To the care of Zakariya was she assigned. Every time that he
... (Her) chamber to see her, He found her supplied with sustenance.
... "O Mary! Whence (comes) this to you?" She said: "From Allah:
... ah Provides sustenance to whom He pleases without measure."

Think not of those who are slain in Allah's way as dead. Nay, they live, finding their sustenance in the presence of their Lord. (3:169)

Jesus, son of Mary, said: O Allah, our Lord, send down to us food from heaven which should be to us an ever-recurring happiness to the first of us and the last of us, and a sign from Thee, and give us sustenance and Thou art the Best of the sustainers. (5:114)

Say: "Come, I will rehearse what Allah hath (really) prohibited you from": Join not anything as equal with Him; be good to your parents; kill not your children on a plea of want; We provide sustenance for you and for them; come not nigh to shameful deeds. Whether open or secret; take not life, which Allah hath made sacred, except by way of justice and law: thus doth He command you, that ye may learn wisdom. (6:151)

Call to mind when ye were a small (band), despised through the land, and afraid that men might despoil and kidnap you; But He provided a safe asylum for you, strengthened you with His aid, and gave you Good things for sustenance: that ye might be grateful. (8:26)

Say: "Who is it that sustains you (in life) from the sky and from the earth? Or who is it that has power over hearing and sight? And who is it that brings out the living from the dead and the dead from the living? And who is it that rules and regulates all affairs?" They will soon say, "Allah". Say, "Will ye not then show piety (to Him)?" (10:31)

We settled the Children of Israel in a beautiful dwelling-place, and provided for them sustenance of the best: it was after knowledge had been granted to them, that they fell into schisms. Verily Allah will judge between them as to the schisms amongst them, on the Day of Judgment. (10:93)

He said: O my people, see you if I have a clear proof from my Lord and He has given me a goodly sustenance from Himself. And I desire not to act in opposition to you, in that which I forbid you. I desire nothing but reform, so far as I am able. And with none but Allah is the direction of my affair to a right issue. In Him I trust and to Him I turn. (11:88)

"O our Lord! I have made some of my offspring to dwell in a valley without cultivation, by Thy Sacred House; in order, O our Lord, that they may establish regular Prayer: so fill the hearts of some among men with love towards them, and feed them with fruits: so that they may give thanks. (14:37)

And Allah has made for you mates (and companions) of your own nature, and made for you, out of them, sons and daughters and grandchildren, and provided for you sustenance of the best: will they then believe in vain things, and be ungrateful for Allah's favours? (16:72)

Allah sets forth the Parable (of two men: one) a slave under the dominion of another; He has no power of any sort; and (the other) a man on whom We have bestowed goodly favours from Ourselves, and he spends thereof (freely), privately and publicly: are the two equal? (By no means;) Praise be to Allah. But most of them understand not. (16:75)

Kill not your children for fear of want: We shall provide sustenance for them as well as for you. Verily the killing of them is a great sin. (17:31)

We have honoured the sons of Adam; provided them with transport on land and sea; given them for sustenance things good and pure; and conferred on them special favours, above a great part of our creation. (17:70)

(Saying): "Eat of the good things We have provided for your sustenance, but commit no excess therein, lest My Wrath should justly descend on you: and those on whom descends My Wrath do perish indeed! (20:81)

Enjoin prayer on thy people, and be constant therein. We ask thee not to provide sustenance: We provide it for thee. But the (fruit of) the Hereafter is for righteousness. (20:132)

That Allah may reward them according to the best of their deeds, and add even more for them out of His Grace: for Allah doth provide for those whom He will, without measure. (24:38)

Or, Who originates creation, then repeats it, and who gives you sustenance from heaven and earth? (Can there be another) god besides Allah? Say, "Bring forth your argument, if ye are telling the truth!" (27:64)

How many are the creatures that carry not their own sustenance? It is Allah who feeds (both) them and you: for He hears and knows (all things). (29:60)

It is Allah Who has created you: further, He has provided for your sustenance; then He will cause you to die; and again He will give you life. Are there any of your (false) "Partners" who can do any single one of these things? Glory to Him! and high is He above the partners they attribute (to him)! (30:40)

Say: "Who gives you sustenance, from the heavens and the earth?" Say: "It is Allah; and certain it is that either we or ye are on right guidance or in manifest error!" (34:24)

O Men, call to mind the favour of Allah to you. Is there any Creator besides Allah who provides for you from the heaven and the earth? There is no God but He. How are you then turned away? (35:3)

He it is Who shows you His signs and sends down for you sustenance from heaven, and none minds but he who turns (to Him). (40:13)

"He that works evil will not be requited but by the like thereof: and he that works a righteous deed - whether man or woman - and is a Believer - such will enter the Garden (of Bliss): Therein will they have abundance without measure. (40:40)

Allah is He Who made the earth a resting-place for you and the heaven a structure, and He formed you, then made goodly your forms, and He provided you with goodly things. That is Allah, your Lord -- so blessed is Allah, the Lord of the worlds. (40:64)

Gracious is Allah to His servants: He gives Sustenance to whom He pleases: and He has power and can carry out His Will. (42:19)

And (in) the variation of the night and the day and (in) the sustenance which Allah sends down from the heaven, then gives life thereby to the earth after its death and (in) the changing of the winds, are signs for a people who understand. (45:5)

And certainly We gave the Children of Israel the Book and judgment and prophethood and provided them with good things, and made them excel the nations. (45:16)

As sustenance for (Allah's) Servants; and We give (new) life therewith to land that is dead: Thus will be the Resurrection. (50:11)

And He provides for him from (sources) he never could imagine. And if any one puts his trust in Allah, sufficient is (Allah) for him. For Allah will surely accomplish his purpose: verily, for all things has Allah appointed a due proportion. (65:3)

It is He Who has made the earth manageable for you, so traverse ye through its tracts and enjoy of the Sustenance which He furnishes: but unto Him is the Resurrection. (67:15)

Who provides them with food against hunger, and with security against fear (of danger). (106:4)

Allah Gives Wealth

But if they disagree (and must part), Allah will provide abundance for all from His all-reaching bounty: for Allah is He that careth for all and is Wise. (4:130)

Marry those among you who are single, or the virtuous ones among yourselves, male or female: if they are in poverty, Allah will give them means out of His grace: for Allah encompasseth all, and he knoweth all things. (24:32)

That it is He Who giveth wealth and satisfaction. (53:48)

And soon will thy Guardian-Lord give thee (that wherewith) thou shalt be well-pleased. Did He not find thee an orphan and give thee shelter (and care)? And He found thee wandering, and He gave thee guidance. And He found thee in need, and made thee independent. (93:5-8)

Allah Gives Without Measure

The life of this world is alluring to those who reject faith, and they scoff at those who believe. But the righteous will be above them on the Day of Resurrection; for Allah bestows His abundance without measure on whom He will. (2:212)

"Thou causest the night to gain on the day, and thou causest the day to gain on the night; Thou bringest the Living out of the dead, and Thou bringest the dead out of the Living; and Thou givest sustenance to whom Thou pleasest, without measure." (3:27)

So her Lord accepted her with a goodly acceptance and made her grow up a goodly growing, and gave her into the charge of Zacharias. Whenever Zacharias entered the sanctuary to (see) her, he found food with her. He said: O Mary, whence comes this to thee? She said: It is from Allah. Surely Allah gives to whom He pleases without measure. (3:37)

That Allah may reward them according to the best of their deeds, and add even more for them out of His Grace: for Allah doth provide for those whom He will, without measure. (24:38)

"He that works evil will not be requited but by the like thereof: and he that works a righteous deed - whether man or woman - and is a Believer- such will enter the Garden (of Bliss): Therein will they have abundance without measure. (40:40)

Gives You Shape And Make Your Shapes Beautiful

He it is Who shapes you in the wombs as He pleases. There is no god but He, the Exalted in Might, the Wise. (3:6)

... Who created you and gave you shape; then We bade the angels
... to Adam, and they prostrate; not so Iblis; He refused to be of
... ho prostrate. (7:11)

... thy Lord said to the angels: "I am about to create man, from
... ig clay from mud moulded into shape; "When I have fashioned
... due proportion) and breathed into him of My spirit, fall ye down
... ance unto him." (15:28-29)

... I have fashioned him (in due proportion) and breathed into him
... pirit, fall ye down in obeisance unto him." (38:72)

... ah Who has made for you the earth as a resting place, and the sky
... opy, and has given you shape - and made your shapes beautiful,
... provided for you Sustenance, of things pure and good; such is
... our Lord. So Glory to Allah, the Lord of the Worlds! (40:64)

... created the heavens and the earth in just proportions, and has
... ou shape, and made your shapes beautiful: and to Him is the final
... 4:3)

... ever Form He wills, does He put thee together. (82:8)

... God In Heaven And On Earth

... Who is Allah in heaven and Allah on earth; and He is full of
... n and Knowledge. (43:84)

... rants Laughter And Tears

... is He Who granteth Laughter and Tears. (53:43)

... uides To Himself Those Who Turn To Him

... ne religion has He established for you as that which He enjoined
... h - the which We have sent by inspiration to thee - and that which
... joined on Abraham, Moses, and Jesus: Namely, that ye should
... steadfast in religion, and make no divisions therein: to those who
... other things than Allah, hard is the (way) to which thou callest

them. Allah chooses to Himself those whom He pleases, and guides to Himself those who turn (to Him). (42:13)

Allah Has Grasp Of Every Creature By Its Forelock

"I put my trust in Allah, My Lord and your Lord! There is not a moving creature, but He hath grasp of its fore-lock. Verily, it is my Lord that is on a straight Path. (11:56)

Let him beware! If he desist not, We will drag him by the forelock, a lying, sinful forelock! (95:15-16)

Allah Has Subjected To You All Things

Among His Signs in this, that He created you from dust; and then, behold, ye are men scattered (far and wide)! (31:20)

Hasten To Allah

Hasten ye then (at once) to Allah: I am from Him a Warner to you, clear and open! (51:50)

Allah Hears Arguments of Husband and Wife

Allah has indeed heard (and accepted) the statement of the woman who pleads with thee concerning her husband and carries her complaint (in prayer) to Allah: and Allah (always) hears the arguments between both sides among you: for Allah hears and sees (all things). (58:1)

Allah Is Not Unjust

These are the Signs of Allah: We rehearse them to thee in Truth: And Allah means no injustice to any of His creatures. (3:108)

What they spend in the life of this (material) world May be likened to a wind which brings a nipping frost: It strikes and destroys the harvest of men who have wronged their own souls: it is not Allah that hath wronged them, but they wrong themselves. (3:117)

This is because of the (unrighteous deeds) which your hands sent on before ye: For Allah never harms those who serve Him. (3:182)

Allah is never unjust in the least degree: If there is any good (done), He doubleth it, and giveth from His own presence a great reward. (4:40)

Because of (the deeds) which your (own) hands sent forth; for Allah is never unjust to His servants. (8:51)

Hath not the story reached them of those before them? The People of Noah, and 'Ad, and Thamud; the People of Abraham, the men of Midian, and the cities overthrown. To them came their messengers with clear signs. It is not Allah Who wrongs them, but they wrong their own souls. (9:70)

Verily Allah will not deal unjustly with man in aught: It is man that wrongs his own soul. (10:44)

And the Book (of Deeds) will be placed (before you); and thou wilt see the sinful in great terror because of what is (recorded) therein; they will say, "Ah! Woe to us! What a Book is this! It leaves out nothing small or great, but takes account thereof!" They will find all that they did, placed before them: And not one will thy Lord treat with injustice. (18:49)

(It will be said): "This is because of the deeds which thy hands sent forth, for verily Allah is not unjust to His servants." (22:10)

Whoever works righteousness benefits his own soul; whoever works evil, it is against his own soul: nor is thy Lord ever unjust (in the least) to His Servants. (41:46)

Nowise shall We be unjust to them: but it is they who have been unjust themselves. (43:76)

"The Word changes not before Me, and I do not the least injustice to My Servants." (50:29)

Allah Is Not Unmindful of What You Do

Thenceforth were your hearts hardened: They became like a rock and even worse in hardness. For among rocks there are some from which rivers gush forth; others there are which when split asunder send forth water; and others which sink for fear of Allah. And Allah is not unmindful of what ye do. (2:74)

After this it is ye, the same people, who slay among yourselves, and banish a party of you from their homes; assist (Their enemies) against them, in guilt and rancour; and if they come to you as captives, ye ransom them, though it was not lawful for you to banish them. Then is it only a part of the Book that ye believe in, and do ye reject the rest? But what is the reward for those among you who behave like this but disgrace in this life? And on the Day of Judgment they shall be consigned to the most grievous penalty. For Allah is not unmindful of what ye do. (2:85)

Or do ye say that Abraham, Ismail, Isaac, Jacob and the Tribes were Jews or Christians? Say: Do ye know better than Allah? Ah! Who is more unjust than those who conceal the testimony they have from Allah? But Allah is not unmindful of what ye do! (2:140)

We see the turning of thy face (for guidance to the heavens: now Shall We turn thee to a Qibla that shall please thee. Turn then Thy face in the direction of the sacred Mosque: Wherever ye are, turn your faces in that direction. The people of the Book know well that that is the truth from their Lord. Nor is Allah unmindful of what they do. (2:144)

From whencesoever Thou startest forth, turn Thy face in the direction of the sacred Mosque; that is indeed the truth from the Lord. And Allah is not unmindful of what ye do. (2:149)

Say: "O ye People of the Book! Why obstruct ye those who believe, from the path of Allah, Seeking to make it crooked, while ye were yourselves witnesses (to Allah's Covenant)? But Allah is not unmindful of all that ye do." (3:99)

To all are degrees (or ranks) according to their deeds: for thy Lord is not unmindful of anything that they do. (6:132)

To Allah do belong the unseen (secrets) of the heavens and the earth, and to Him goeth back every affair (for decision): then worship Him, and put thy trust in Him: and thy Lord is not unmindful of aught that ye do. (11:123)

Think not that Allah doth not heed the deeds of those who do wrong. He but giveth them respite against a Day when the eyes will fixedly stare in horror. (14:42)

Fulfill the Covenant of Allah when ye have entered into it, and break not your oaths after ye have confirmed them; indeed ye have made Allah your surety; for Allah knoweth all that ye do. (16:91)

If they do wrangle with thee, say, "Allah knows best what it is ye are doing." (22:68)

And We have made, above you, seven tracts; and We are never unmindful of (our) Creation. (23:17)

And say: "Praise be to Allah, Who will soon show you His Signs, so that ye shall know them"; and thy Lord is not unmindful of all that ye do. (27:93)

Allah Is Sufficient

So if they believe as ye believe, they are indeed on the right path; but if they turn back, it is they who are in schism; but Allah will suffice thee as against them, and He is the All-Hearing, the All-Knowing. (2:137)

Men said to them: "A great army is gathering against you": And frightened them: But it (only) increased their Faith: They said: "For us Allah sufficeth, and He is the best disposer of affairs." (3:173)

Make trial of orphans until they reach the age of marriage; if then ye find sound judgment in them, release their property to them; but consume it not wastefully, nor in haste against their growing up. If the guardian is well-off, let him claim no remuneration, but if he is poor, let him have for himself what is just and reasonable. When ye release their property to them, take witnesses in their presence: But all-sufficient is Allah in taking account. (4:6)

But Allah hath full knowledge of your enemies: Allah is enough for a protector, and Allah is enough for a Helper. (4:45)

Such is the bounty from Allah: And sufficient is it that Allah knoweth all. (4:70)

They have "Obedience" on their lips; but when they leave thee, a section of them Meditate all night on things very different from what thou tellest them. But Allah records their nightly (plots): So keep clear of them, and put thy trust in Allah, and enough is Allah as a disposer of affairs. (4:81)

Yea, unto Allah belong all things in the heavens and on earth, and enough is Allah to carry through all affairs. (4:132)

But Allah beareth witness that what He hath sent unto thee He hath sent from His (own) knowledge, and the angels bear witness: But enough is Allah for a witness. (4:166)

O People of the Book! Commit no excesses in your religion: Nor say of Allah aught but the truth. Christ Jesus the son of Mary was (no more than) a messenger of Allah, and His Word, which He bestowed on Mary, and a spirit proceeding from Him: so believe in Allah and His messengers. Say not "Trinity": desist: it will be better for you: for Allah is one Allah: Glory be to Him: (far exalted is He) above having a son. To Him belong all things in the heavens and on earth. And enough is Allah as a Disposer of affairs. (4:171)

Should they intend to deceive thee, verily Allah sufficeth thee: He it is That hath strengthened thee with His aid and with (the company of) the Believers. (8:62)

O Prophet! Sufficient unto thee is Allah, (unto thee) and unto those who follow thee among the Believers. (8:64)

If only they had been content with what Allah and His Messenger gave them, and had said, "Sufficient unto us is Allah! Allah and His Messenger will soon give us of His bounty: to Allah do we turn our hopes!" (That would have been the right course.) (9:59)

they turn away, Say: "Allah sufficeth me: there is no god but He:
in is my trust, He the Lord of the Throne (of Glory) Supreme!"

h is Allah for a witness between us and you: we certainly knew
of your worship of us!" (10:29)

believers say: "No messenger art thou." Say: "Enough for a
between me and you is Allah, and such as have knowledge of
k." (13:43)

ficient are We unto thee against those who scoff. (15:95)

any generations have We destroyed after Noah? And enough is
d to note and see the sins of His servants. (17:17)

My servants, no authority shalt thou have over them:" Enough is
d for a Disposer of affairs. (17:65)

nough is Allah for a witness between me and you: for He is well
ted with His servants, and He sees (all things). (17:96)

ve We made for every prophet an enemy among the sinners: but
is thy Lord to guide and to help. (25:31)

ly on the Ever-Living Who dies not, and celebrate His praise. And
nt is He as being Aware of His servants' sins. (25:58)

lah is sufficient as a witness between me and you - He knows
in the heavens and the earth. And those who believe in falsehood
believe in Allah, these it is that are the losers. (29:52)

t thy trust in Allah, and enough is Allah as a disposer of affairs.

And Allah turned back the Unbelievers for (all) their fury: no advantage did they gain; and enough is Allah for the believers in their fight. And Allah is full of Strength, able to enforce His Will. (33:25)

(It is the practice of those) who preach the Messages of Allah, and fear Him, and fear none but Allah. And enough is Allah to call (men) to account. (33:39)

And obey not (the behests) of the Unbelievers and the Hypocrites, and heed not their annoyances, but put thy Trust in Allah. For enough is Allah as a Disposer of affairs. (33:48)

Is not Allah enough for his Servant? But they try to frighten thee with other (gods) besides Him! For such as Allah leaves to stray, there can be no guide. (39:36)

If indeed thou ask them who it is that created the heavens and the earth, they would be sure to say, "Allah". Say: "See ye then? The things that ye invoke besides Allah, can they, if Allah wills some Penalty for me, remove His Penalty? Or if He wills some Grace for me, can they keep back his Grace?" Say: "Sufficient is Allah for me! In Him trust those who put their trust." (39:38)

Or do they say, "He has forged it"? Say: "Had I forged it, then can ye obtain no single (blessing) for me from Allah. He knows best of that whereof ye talk (so glibly)! Enough is He for a witness between me and you! And he is Oft-Forgiving, Most Merciful." (46:8)

It is He Who has sent His Messenger with Guidance and the Religion of Truth, to proclaim it over all religion: and enough is Allah for a Witness. (48:28)

And He provides for him from (sources) he never could imagine. And if any one puts his trust in Allah, sufficient is (Allah) for him. For Allah will surely accomplish his purpose: verily, for all things has Allah appointed a due proportion. (65:3)

Allah Is The Best Of Planners

And (the unbelievers) plotted and planned, and Allah too planned, and the best of planners is Allah. (3:54)

Remember how the Unbelievers plotted against thee, to keep thee in bonds, or slay thee, or get thee out (of thy home). They plot and plan, and Allah too plans; but the best of planners is Allah. (8:30)

Those before them did (also) devise plots; but in all things the master-planning is Allah's. He knoweth the doings of every soul: and soon will the Unbelievers know who gets home in the end. (13:42)

Allah Is With You Wheresoever You May Be

He it is Who created the heavens and the earth in Six Days, and is moreover firmly established on the Throne (of Authority). He knows what enters within the earth and what comes forth out of it, what comes down from heaven and what mounts up to it. And He is with you wheresoever ye may be. And Allah sees well all that ye do. (57:4)

Seest thou not that Allah doth know (all) that is in the heavens and on earth? There is not a secret consultation between three, but He makes the fourth among them, Nor between five but He makes the sixth, nor between fewer nor more, but He is in their midst, wheresoever they be: In the end will He tell them the truth of their conduct, on the Day of Judgment. For Allah has full knowledge of all things. (58:7)

Allah Knows What You Reveal And What You Conceal

Know they not that Allah knoweth what they conceal and what they reveal? (2:77)

Say: "Whether ye hide what is in your hearts or reveal it, Allah knows it all: He knows what is in the heavens, and what is on earth. And Allah has power over all things. (3:29)

The Messenger's duty is but to proclaim (the message). But Allah knoweth all that ye reveal and ye conceal. (5:99)

He it is created you from clay, and then decreed a stated term (for you). And there is in His presence another determined term; yet ye doubt within yourselves! (6:2)

Behold! They fold up their hearts, that they may lie hid from Him! Ah even when they cover themselves with their garments, He knoweth what they conceal, and what they reveal: for He knoweth well the (inmost secrets) of the hearts. (11:5)

"O our Lord! Truly Thou dost know what we conceal and what we reveal: for nothing whatever is hidden from Allah, whether on earth or in heaven. (14:38)

And Allah doth know what ye conceal, and what ye reveal. (16:19)

Undoubtedly Allah doth know what they conceal, and what they reveal: verily He loveth not the arrogant. (16:23)

(Kept them away from the Path), that they should not worship Allah, Who brings to light what is hidden in the heavens and the earth, and knows what ye hide and what ye reveal. (27:25)

And verily thy Lord knoweth all that their hearts do hide. As well as all that they reveal. (27:74)

And thy Lord knows all that their hearts conceal and all that they reveal. (28:69)

Whether ye reveal anything or conceal it, verily Allah has full knowledge of all things. (33:54)

Let not their speech, then, grieve thee. Verily We know what they hide as well as what they disclose. (36:76)

Those who avoid great sins and shameful deeds, only (falling into) small faults, verily thy Lord is ample in forgiveness. He knows you well when He brings you out of the earth, And when ye are hidden in your mothers' wombs. Therefore justify not yourselves: He knows best who it is that guards against evil. (53:32)

O ye who believe! Take not my enemies and yours as friends (or protectors), offering them (your) love, even though they have rejected the Truth that has come to you, and have (on the contrary) driven out the Prophet and yourselves (from your homes), (simply) because ye believe in Allah your Lord! If ye have come out to strive in My Way and to seek My Good Pleasure, (take them not as friends), holding secret converse of love (and friendship) with them: for I know full well all that ye conceal and all that ye reveal. And any of you that does this has strayed from the Straight Path. (60:1)

He knows what is in the heavens and on earth; and He knows what ye conceal and what ye reveal: yea, Allah knows well the (secrets) of (all) hearts. (64:4)

Allah Knows The Secret Of The Heart

Say: "Whether ye hide what is in your hearts or reveal it, Allah knows it all: He knows what is in the heavens, and what is on earth. And Allah has power over all things. (3:29)

Ah! ye are those who love them, but they love you not, though ye believe in the whole of the Book. When they meet you, they say, "We believe": But when they are alone, they bite off the very tips of their fingers at you in their rage. Say: "Perish in you rage; Allah knoweth well all the secrets of the heart." (3:119)

After (the excitement) of the distress, He sent down calm on a band of you overcome with slumber, while another band was stirred to anxiety by their own feelings, moved by wrong suspicions of Allah-suspicions due to ignorance. They said: "What affair is this of ours?" Say thou: "Indeed, this affair is wholly Allah's." They hide in their minds what they dare not reveal to thee. They say (to themselves): "If we had had anything to do with this affair, We should not have been in the slaughter here." Say: "Even if you had remained in your homes, those for whom death was decreed would certainly have gone forth to the place of their death"; but (all this was) that Allah might test what is in your breasts and purge what is in your hearts. For Allah knoweth well the secrets of your hearts. (3:154)

And call in remembrance the favour of Allah unto you, and His covenant, which He ratified with you, when ye said: "We hear and we obey": And fear Allah, for Allah knoweth well the secrets of your hearts. (5:7)

Remember in thy dream Allah showed them to thee as few: if He had shown them to thee as many, ye would surely have been discouraged, and ye would surely have disputed in (your) decision; but Allah saved (you): for He knoweth well the (secrets) of (all) hearts. (8:43)

Behold! They fold up their hearts, that they may lie hid from Him! Ah even when they cover themselves with their garments, He knoweth what they conceal, and what they reveal: for He knoweth well the (inmost secrets) of the hearts. (11:5)

And thy Lord knows all that their hearts conceal and all that they reveal. (28:69)

Then there are among men such as say, "We believe in Allah"; but when they suffer affliction in (the cause of) Allah, they treat men's oppression as if it were the Wrath of Allah! And if help comes (to thee) from thy Lord, they are sure to say, "We have (always) been with you!" Does not Allah know best all that is in the hearts of all creation? (29:10)

Thou mayest defer (the turn of) any of them that thou pleasest, and thou mayest receive any thou pleasest: and there is no blame on thee if thou invite one whose (turn) thou hadst set aside. This were nigher to the cooling of their eyes, the prevention of their grief, and their satisfaction - that of all of them - with that which thou hast to give them: and Allah knows (all) that is in your hearts: and Allah is All-Knowing, Most Forbearing. (33:51)

Verily Allah knows (all) the hidden things of the heavens and the earth: verily He has full knowledge of all that is in (men's) hearts. (35:38)

ject (Allah), Truly Allah hath no need of you; but He liketh not
ude from His servants: if ye are grateful, He is pleased with you.
er of burdens can bear the burden of another. In the end, to your
your Return, when He will tell you the truth of all that ye did (in
). For He knoweth well all that is in (men's) hearts. (39:7)

knows of (the tricks) that deceive with the eyes, and all that the
of men) conceal. (40:19)

Do they say, "He has forged a falsehood against Allah"? But if
illed, He could seal up thy heart. And Allah blots out Vanity, and
the Truth by His Words. For He knows well the secrets of all
(42:24)

We Who created man, and We know what dark suggestions his
akes to him: for We are nearer to him than (his) jugular vein.

ges Night into Day, and He merges Day into Night; and He has
wledge of the secrets of (all) hearts. (57:6)

nether ye hide your word or publish it, He certainly has (full)
ledge, of the secrets of (all) hearts. Should He not know, He that
? And He is the One that understands the finest mysteries (and) is
quainted (with them). (67:13-14)

lah has full knowledge of what they secrete (in their breasts).

Knows What Is Hidden

will Allah gather the messengers together, and ask: "What was
onse ye received (from men to your teaching)?" They will say:
ve no knowledge: it is Thou Who knowest in full all that is
" (5:109)

hold! Allah will say: "O Jesus the son of Mary! Didst thou say
n, worship me and my mother as gods in derogation of Allah'?"
say: "Glory to Thee! Never could I say what I had no right (to

say). Had I said such a thing, thou wouldst indeed have known it. Thou knowest what is in my heart, Thou I know not what is in Thine. For Thou knowest in full all that is hidden. (5:116)

With Him are the keys of the unseen, the treasures that none knoweth but He. He knoweth whatever there is on the earth and in the sea. Not a leaf doth fall but with His knowledge: there is not a grain in the darkness (or depths) of the earth, nor anything fresh or dry (green or withered), but is (inscribed) in a record clear (to those who can read). (6:59)

It is He who created the heavens and the earth in true (proportions): the day He saith, "Be." Behold! It is. His word is the truth. His will be the dominion the day the trumpet will be blown. He knoweth the unseen as well as that which is open. For He is the Wise, well acquainted (with all things). (6:73)

Know they not that Allah doth know their secret (thoughts) and their secret counsels, and that Allah knoweth well all things unseen? (9:78)

They will present their excuses to you when ye return to them. Say thou: "Present no excuses: we shall not believe you: Allah hath already informed us of the true state of matters concerning you: It is your actions that Allah and His Messenger will observe: in the end will ye be brought back to Him Who knoweth what is hidden and what is open: then will He show you the truth of all that ye did." (9:94)

And say: "Work (righteousness): Soon will Allah observe your work, and His Messenger, and the Believers: Soon will ye be brought back to the knower of what is hidden and what is open: then will He show you the truth of all that ye did." (9:105)

They say: "Why is not a sign sent down to him from his Lord?" Say: "The Unseen is only for Allah (to know), then wait ye: I too will wait with you." (10:20)

To Allah do belong the unseen (secrets) of the heavens and the earth, and to Him goeth back every affair (for decision): then worship Him, and put thy trust in Him: and thy Lord is not unmindful of aught that ye do. (11:123)

He knoweth the unseen and that which is open: He is the Great, the Most High. It is the same (to Him) whether any of you conceal his speech or declare it openly; whether he lie hid by night or walk forth freely by day. (13:9-10)

To Allah belongeth the Mystery of the heavens and the earth. And the Decision of the Hour (of Judgment) is as the twinkling of an eye, or even quicker: for Allah hath power over all things. (16:77)

Say: "Allah knows best how long they stayed: with Him is (the knowledge of) the secrets of the heavens and the earth: how clearly He sees, how finely He hears (everything)! They have no protector other than Him; nor does He share His Command with any person whatsoever. (18:26)

If thou pronounce the word aloud, (it is no matter): for verily He knoweth what is secret and what is yet more hidden. (20:7)

It is He Who knows what is open in speech and what ye hide (in your hearts). (21:110)

He knows what is hidden and what is open: too high is He for the partners they attribute to Him! (23:92)

Say: "The (Qur'an) was sent down by Him who knows the mystery (that is) in the heavens and the earth: verily He is Oft-Forgiving, Most Merciful." (25:6)

Say: "None in the heavens or on earth, except Allah, knows what is hidden: nor can they perceive when they shall be raised up (for Judgment)." (27:65)

Such is He, the Knower of all things, hidden and open, the Exalted (in power), the Merciful. (32:6)

The Unbelievers say, "Never to us will come the Hour": Say, "Nay! but most surely, by my Lord, it will come upon you;- by Him Who knows the unseen, from Whom is not hidden the least little atom in the heavens or on earth: Nor is there anything less than that, or greater, but is in the Record Perspicuous. "(34:3)

Say: "Verily my Lord doth cast the (mantle of) Truth (over His servants), He that has full knowledge of (all) that is hidden." (34:48)

"Verily Allah knows the secrets of the heavens and the earth: and Allah Sees well all that ye do." (49:18)

"He (alone) knows the Unseen, nor does He make any one acquainted with His Mysteries, except a messenger whom He has chosen: and then He makes a band of watchers march before him and behind him, that He may know that they have (truly) brought and delivered the Messages of their Lord: and He surrounds (all the mysteries) that are with them, and takes account of every single thing." (72:26-28)

Except as Allah wills: For He knoweth what is manifest and what is hidden. (87:7)

Allah Listens To The Distressed

Or, Who listens to the (soul) distressed when it calls on Him, and Who relieves its suffering, and makes you (mankind) inheritors of the earth? (Can there be another) god besides Allah? Little it is that ye heed! (27:62)

Allah Listens To The Believers And The Doers of Good

And He listens to those who believe and do deeds of righteousness, and gives them increase of His Bounty: but for the Unbelievers their is a terrible Penalty. (42:26)

Allah Loves The Righteous

(But the treaties are) not dissolved with those Pagans with whom ye have entered into alliance and who have not subsequently failed you in aught, nor aided any one against you. So fulfill your engagements with them to the end of their term: for Allah loveth the righteous. (9:4)

How can there be an agreement for the idolaters with Allah and with his Messenger, except those with whom you made an agreement at the Sacred Mosque? So as long as they are true to you, be true to them. Surely Allah loves those who keep their duty. (9:7)

On those who believe and work deeds of righteousness, will (Allah) Most Gracious bestow love. (19:96)

And spend of your substance in the cause of Allah, and make not your own hands contribute to (your) destruction; but do good; for Allah loveth those who do good. (2:195)

Those who spend (freely), whether in prosperity, or in adversity; who restrain anger, and pardon (all) men; for Allah loves those who do good. (3:134)

And Allah gave them a reward in this world, and the excellent reward of the Hereafter. For Allah Loveth those who do good. (3:148)

But because of their breach of their covenant, We cursed them, and made their hearts grow hard; they change the words from their (right) places and forget a good part of the message that was sent them, nor wilt thou cease to find them - barring a few - ever bent on (new) deceits: but forgive them, and overlook (their misdeeds): for Allah loveth those who are kind. (5:13)

On those who believe and do deeds of righteousness there is no blame for what they ate (in the past), when they guard themselves from evil, and believe, and do deeds of righteousness, (or) again, guard themselves from evil and believe, (or) again, guard themselves from evil and do good. For Allah loveth those who do good. (5:93)

On that day those who reject Faith and disobey the messenger will wish that the earth were made one with them: But never will they hide a single fact from Allah! (4:42)

If two parties among the Believers fall into a quarrel, make ye peace between them: but if one of them transgresses beyond bounds against the other, then fight ye (all) against the one that transgresses until it complies with the command of Allah; but if it complies, then make peace between them with justice, and be fair: for Allah loves those who are fair (and just). (49:9)

Allah forbids you not, with regard to those who fight you not for (your) Faith nor drive you out of your homes, from dealing kindly and justly with them: for Allah loveth those who are just. (60:8)

Truly Allah loves those who fight in His Cause in battle array, as if they were a solid cemented structure. (61:4)

They ask thee concerning women's courses. Say: They are a hurt and a pollution. So keep away from women in their courses, and do not approach them until they are clean. But when they have purified themselves, ye may approach them in any manner, time, or place ordained for you by Allah. For Allah loves those who turn to Him constantly and He loves those who keep themselves pure and clean. (2:222)

Never stand thou forth therein. There is a mosque whose foundation was laid from the first day on piety; it is more worthy of the standing forth (for prayer) therein. In it are men who love to be purified; and Allah loveth those who make themselves pure. (9:108)

It is part of the Mercy of Allah that thou dost deal gently with them. Wert thou severe or harsh-hearted, they would have broken away from about thee: so pass over (Their faults), and ask for (Allah's) forgiveness for them; and consult them in affairs (of moment). Then, when thou hast Taken a decision put thy trust in Allah. For Allah loves those who put their trust (in Him). (3:159)

Allah Never Breaks His Promise

"Our Lord! Thou art He that will gather mankind Together against a day about which there is no doubt; for Allah never fails in His promise." (3:9)

ord! Grant us what Thou didst promise unto us through Thine
gers, and save us from shame on the Day of Judgment: For Thou
reakest Thy promise." (3:194)

there could be a Qur'an with which the mountains were made to
ay, or the earth were cloven asunder, or the dead were made to
nay, the commandment is wholly Allah's. Do not those who
know that, if Allah please, He would certainly guide all the
And as for those who disbelieve, disaster will not cease to afflict
cause of what they do, or it will alight close by their abodes, until
mise of Allah come to pass. Surely Allah will not fail in (His)
(13:31)

think that Allah would fail his messengers in His promise: for
Exalted in power, - the Lord of Retribution. (14:47)

he promise of Allah. Never does Allah depart from His promise:
t men understand not. (30:6)

llah

ey Allah and the Messenger; that ye may obtain mercy. (3:132)

who believe, obey Allah and obey the Messenger and those in
ty from among you; then if you quarrel about any thing, refer it to
nd the Messenger, if you believe in Allah and the Last Day. This
and more suitable to (achieve) the end. (4:59)

obey Allah and the messenger are in the company of those on
is the Grace of Allah, of the prophets (who teach), the sincere
of Truth), the witnesses (who testify), and the Righteous (who do
Ah! what a beautiful fellowship! (4:69)

k thee concerning (things taken as) spoils of war. Say: "(Such)
re at the disposal of Allah and the Messenger: So fear Allah, and
raight the relations between yourselves: Obey Allah and His
ger, if ye do believe." (8:1)

O ye who believe! Obey Allah and His Messenger, and turn not away from him when ye hear (him speak). Nor be like those who say, "We hear," but listen not. (8:20-21)

And obey Allah and His Messenger and dispute not one with another, lest you get weak-hearted and your power depart; and be steadfast. Surely Allah is with the steadfast. (8:46)

And the believers, men and women, are friends one of another. They enjoin good and forbid evil and keep up prayer and pay the poor-rate, and obey Allah and His Messenger. As for these, Allah will have mercy on them. Surely Allah is Mighty, Wise. (9:71)

The response of the believers, when they are invited to Allah and His Messenger that he may judge between them, is only that they say: We hear and we obey. And these it is that are successful. And he who obeys Allah and His Messenger, and fears Allah and keeps duty to Him, these it is that are the achievers. And they swear by Allah with their strongest oaths that, if thou command them, they would certainly go forth. Say: Swear not; reasonable obedience (is desired). Surely Allah is Aware of what you do. Say: Obey Allah and obey the Messenger. But if you turn away, he is responsible for the duty imposed on him, and you are responsible for the duty imposed on you. And if you obey him, you go aright. And the Messenger's duty is only to deliver (the message) plainly. (24:51-54)

And stay in your houses and display not your beauty like the displaying of the ignorance of yore; and keep up prayer, and pay the poor-rate, and obey Allah and His Messenger. Allah only desires to take away uncleanness from you, O people of the household, and to purify you a (thorough) purifying. (33:33)

He will put your deeds into a right state for you, and forgive you your sins. And whoever obeys Allah and His Messenger, he indeed achieves a mighty success. (33:71)

Obedience and a gentle word (was proper). Then when the affair is settled, it is better for them if they remain true to Allah. (47:21)

O you who believe, obey Allah and obey the Messenger and make not your deeds vain. (47:33)

Say to the desert Arabs who lagged behind: "Ye shall be summoned (to fight) against a people given to vehement war: then shall ye fight, or they shall submit. Then if ye show obedience, Allah will grant you a goodly reward, but if ye turn back as ye did before, He will punish you with a grievous Penalty." No blame is there on the blind, nor is there blame on the lame, nor on one ill (if he joins not the war): But he that obeys Allah and his Messenger, (Allah) will admit him to Gardens beneath which rivers flow; and he who turns back, (Allah) will punish him with a grievous Penalty. (48:16-17)

The desert Arabs say, "We believe." Say, "Ye have no faith; but ye (only) say, 'We have submitted our wills to Allah,' For not yet has Faith entered your hearts. But if ye obey Allah and His Messenger, He will not belittle aught of your deeds: for Allah is Oft-Forgiving, Most Merciful." (49:14)

Do you fear that you will not (be able to) give in charity before your consultation? So when you do it not, and Allah has turned to you (mercifully), keep up prayer and pay the poor-rate and obey Allah and His Messenger. And Allah is Aware of what you do. (58:13)

So obey Allah, and obey His Messenger: but if ye turn back, the duty of Our Messenger is but to proclaim (the Message) clearly and openly. (64:12)

So fear Allah as much as ye can; listen and obey and spend in charity for the benefit of your own soul and those saved from the covetousness of their own souls, they are the ones that achieve prosperity. (64:16)

Prepares A Way Out and Provides Unimaginable Sources

So when they have reached their prescribed time, retain them with kindness or dismiss them with kindness, and call to witness two just ones from among you, and give upright testimony for Allah. With that is admonished he who believes in Allah and the Latter day. And whoever keeps his duty to Allah, He ordains a way out for him, and gives him sustenance from whence he imagines not. And whoever trusts in Allah, He is sufficient for him. Surely Allah attains His purpose. Allah indeed has appointed a measure for everything. (65:2-3)

Raises To Ranks (Degrees)

Those messengers We endowed with gifts, some above others: To one of them Allah spoke; others He raised to degrees (of honour); to Jesus the son of Mary We gave clear (Signs), and strengthened him with the holy spirit. If Allah had so willed, succeeding generations would not have fought among each other, after clear (Signs) had come to them, but they (chose) to wrangle, some believing and others rejecting. If Allah had so willed, they would not have fought each other; but Allah Fulfilleth His plan. (2:253)

There are grades with Allah. And Allah is Seer of what they do. (3:163)

(High) degrees from Him and protection and mercy. And Allah is ever Forgiving, Merciful. (4:96)

That was the reasoning about Us, which We gave to Abraham (to use) against his people: We raise whom We will, degree after degree: for thy Lord is full of wisdom and knowledge. (6:83)

To all are degrees (or ranks) according to their deeds: for thy Lord is not unmindful of anything that they do. (6:132)

It is He Who hath made you (His) agents, inheritors of the earth: He hath raised you in ranks, some above others: that He may try you in the gifts He hath given you: for thy Lord is quick in punishment: yet He is indeed Oft-forgiving, Most Merciful. (6:165)

These are the believers in truth. For them are with their Lord exalted grades and protection and an honourable sustenance. (8:4)

So he began (the search) with their baggage, before (he came to) the baggage of his brother: at length he brought it out of his brother's baggage. Thus did We plan for Joseph. He could not take his brother by the law of the king except that Allah willed it (so). We raise to degrees (of wisdom) whom We please: but over all endued with knowledge is one, the All-Knowing. (12:76)

But such as come to Him as Believers who have worked righteous deeds,-for them are ranks exalted. (20:75)

Do they apportion the mercy of thy Lord? We portion out among them their livelihood in the life of this world and We exalt some of them above others in rank, that some of them may take others in service. And the mercy of thy Lord is better than that which they amass. (43:32)

And for all are degrees according to what they do, and that He may pay them for their deeds and they will not be wronged. (46:19)

O you who believe, when it is said to you, Make room in assemblies, make room. Allah will give you ample. And when it is said, rise up, rise up. Allah will exalt those of you who believe, and those who are given knowledge, to high ranks. And Allah is Aware of what you do. (58:11)

Allah Regulates Affairs

Verily your Lord is Allah, who created the heavens and the earth in six days, and is firmly established on the throne (of authority), regulating and governing all things. No intercessor (can plead with Him) except after His leave (hath been obtained). This is Allah your Lord; Him therefore serve ye: will ye not receive admonition? (10:3)

Say: "Who is it that sustains you (in life) from the sky and from the earth? Or who is it that has power over hearing and sight? And who is it that brings out the living from the dead and the dead from the living? And who is it that rules and regulates all affairs?" They will soon say, "Allah". Say, "Will ye not then show piety (to Him)?" (10:31)

Allah is He who raised the heavens without any pillars that you can see, and He is established on the Throne of Power, and He made the sun and the moon subservient (to you). Each one runs to an appointed term. He regulates the affair, making clear the messages that you may be certain of the meeting with your Lord. (13:2)

He orders the Affair from the heaven to the earth; then it will ascend to Him in a day the measure of which is a thousand years as you count. (32:5)

Seek Allah's Forgiveness

The Messenger believeth in what hath been revealed to him from his Lord, as do the men of faith. Each one (of them) believeth in Allah, His angels, His books, and His messengers. "We make no distinction (they say) between one and another of His messengers." And they say: "We hear, and we obey: (We seek) Thy forgiveness, our Lord, and to Thee is the end of all journeys." On no soul doth Allah Place a burden greater than it can bear. It gets every good that it earns, and it suffers every ill that it earns. (Pray:) "Our Lord! Condemn us not if we forget or fall into error; our Lord! Lay not on us a burden Like that which Thou didst lay on those before us; Our Lord! Lay not on us a burden greater than we have strength to bear. Blot out our sins, and grant us forgiveness. Have mercy on us. Thou art our Protector; Help us against those who stand against faith." (2:285-286)

Those who say: Our Lord, we believe, so forgive our sins and save us from the chastisement of the fire. (3:16)

And those who, when they commit an indecency or wrong their souls, remember Allah and ask forgiveness for their sins. And who forgives sins but Allah? And they persist not knowingly in what they do. (3:135)

All that they said was: "Our Lord! Forgive us our sins and anything We may have done that transgressed our duty: Establish our feet firmly, and help us against those that resist Faith." (3:147)

"Our Lord! We have heard the call of one calling (Us) to Faith, 'Believe ye in the Lord,' and we have believed. Our Lord! Forgive us our sins, blot out from us our iniquities, and take to Thyself our souls in the company of the righteous. (3:193)

We sent not a messenger, but to be obeyed, in accordance with the will of Allah. If they had only, when they were unjust to themselves, come unto thee and asked Allah's forgiveness, and the Messenger had asked ness for them, they would have found Allah indeed Oft-returning, Merciful. (4:64)

rn they not to Allah, and seek His forgiveness? For Allah is Oft-ng, Most Merciful. (5:74)

prayed: "O my Lord! Forgive me and my brother! Admit us to rcy! For Thou art the Most Merciful of those who show mercy!"

ses chose seventy of his people for Our place of meeting: when re seized with violent quaking, he prayed: "O my Lord! If it had y will Thou couldst have destroyed, long before, both them and uldst Thou destroy us for the deeds of the foolish ones among us? no more than Thy trial: by it Thou causest whom Thou wilt to nd Thou leadest whom Thou wilt into the right path. Thou art our or: so forgive us and give us Thy mercy; for Thou art the best of ho forgive. (7:155)

o preach thus), 'Seek ye the forgiveness of your Lord, and turn to repentance; that He may grant you enjoyment, good (and true), m appointed, and bestow His abounding grace on all who abound ! But if ye turn away, then I fear for you the penalty of a great 1:3)

my people! Ask forgiveness of your Lord, and turn to Him (in nce): He will send you the skies pouring abundant rain, and add h to your strength: so turn ye not back in sin!" (11:52)

k forgiveness of your Lord, and turn unto Him (in repentance): Lord is indeed full of mercy and loving-kindness." (11:90)

Thamud People (We sent) Salih, one of their own brethren. He) my people! Worship Allah: ye have no other god but Him. It is o hath produced you from the earth and settled you therein: then giveness of Him, and turn to Him (in repentance): for my Lord is) near, ready to answer." (11:61)

"O Joseph, pass this over! (O wife), ask forgiveness for thy sin, for truly thou hast been at fault!" (12:29)

He said: "Soon will I ask my Lord for forgiveness for you: for he is indeed Oft-Forgiving, Most Merciful." (12:98)

"O our Lord! Cover (us) with Thy Forgiveness - me, my parents, and (all) Believers, on the Day that the Reckoning will be established! (14:41)

Abraham said: "Peace be on thee: I will pray to my Lord for thy forgiveness: for He is to me Most Gracious. (19:47)

"A part of My servants there was, who used to pray 'our Lord! We believe; then do Thou forgive us, and have mercy upon us: For Thou art the Best of those who show mercy!" (23:109)

So say: "O my Lord! Grant Thou forgiveness and mercy for Thou art the Best of those who show mercy!" (23:118)

Only those are believers, who believe in Allah and His Messenger: when they are with him on a matter requiring collective action, they do not depart until they have asked for his leave; those who ask for thy leave are those who believe in Allah and His Messenger; so when they ask for thy leave, for some business of theirs, give leave to those of them whom thou wilt, and ask Allah for their forgiveness: for Allah is Oft-Forgiving, Most Merciful. (24:62)

He prayed: "O my Lord! I have indeed wronged my soul! Do Thou then forgive me!" So (Allah) forgave him: for He is the Oft-Forgiving, Most Merciful. (28:16)

Patiently, then, persevere: for the Promise of Allah is true: and ask forgiveness for thy fault, and celebrate the Praises of thy Lord in the evening and in the morning. (40:55)

Say thou: "I am but a man like you: It is revealed to me by Inspiration, that your Allah is one Allah: so stand true to Him, and ask for His Forgiveness." And woe to those who join gods with Allah. (41:6)

Know, therefore, that there is no god but Allah, and ask forgiveness for thy fault, and for the men and women who believe: for Allah knows how ye move about and how ye dwell in your homes. (47:19)

Those of the dwellers of the desert who lagged behind will say to thee: Our property and our families kept us busy, so ask forgiveness for us. They say with their tongues what is not in their hearts. Say: Then who can control aught for you from Allah, if He intends to do you harm or if He intends to do you good. Nay, Allah is ever Aware of what you do. (48:11)

And in the hour of early dawn, they (were found) praying for Forgiveness. (51:18)

"Our Lord! Make us not a (test and) trial for the Unbelievers, but forgive us, our Lord! For Thou art the Exalted in Might, the Wise." (60:5)

O ye who believe! Turn to Allah with sincere repentance: In the hope that your Lord will remove from you your ills and admit you to Gardens beneath which Rivers flow, the Day that Allah will not permit to be humiliated the Prophet and those who believe with him. Their Light will run forward before them and by their right hands, while they say, "Our Lord! Perfect our Light for us, and grant us Forgiveness: for Thou hast power over all things." (66:8)

So I have said: Ask forgiveness of your Lord; surely He is ever Forgiving. (71:10)

"O my Lord! Forgive me, my parents, all who enter my house in Faith, and (all) believing men and believing women: and to the wrong-doers grant Thou no increase but in perdition!" (71:28)

Thy Lord knows indeed that thou passest in prayer nearly two-thirds of the night, and (sometimes) half of it, and (sometimes) a third of it, as do a party of those with thee. And Allah measures the night and the day. He knows that (all of) you are not able to do it, so He has turned to you (mercifully); so read of the Qur'an that which is easy for you. He knows that there are sick among you, and others who travel in the land seeking of Allah's bounty, and others who fight in Allah's way. So read as much of it as is easy (for you), and keep up prayer and pay the poor-rate and offer to Allah a goodly fight. And whatever of good you send on beforehand for yourselves, you will find it with Allah -- that is best and greatest in reward. And ask forgiveness of Allah. Surely Allah is Forgiving, Merciful. (73:20)

Celebrate the praises of thy Lord, and pray for His Forgiveness: For He is Oft-Returning (in Grace and Mercy). (110:3)

Seek Allah's Help

Thee do we worship, and Thine aid we seek. (1:5)

Nay, seek (Allah's) help with patient perseverance and prayer: It is indeed hard, except to those who bring a lowly spirit. (2:45)

O ye who believe! Seek help with patient perseverance and prayer; for Allah is with those who patiently persevere. (2:153)

Say: "O my Lord! Let my entry be by the Gate of Truth and Honour, and likewise my exit by the Gate of Truth and Honour; and grant me from Thy Presence an authority to aid (me)." (17:80)

Seek Refuge In Allah

If a suggestion from Satan assail thy (mind), seek refuge with Allah; for He heareth and knoweth (all things). Those who fear Allah, when a thought of evil from Satan assaults them, bring Allah to remembrance, when lo! They see (aright)! (7:200-201)

Then the word went forth: "O earth! Swallow up thy water, and O sky! Withhold (thy rain)!" and the water abated, and the matter was ended. The Ark rested on Mount Judi, and the word went forth: "Away with those who do wrong!" (11:44)

When thou dost read the Qur'an, seek Allah's protection from Satan the rejected one. (16:98)

She said: "I seek refuge from thee to (Allah) Most Gracious: (come not near) if thou dost fear Allah." (19:18)

And say "O my Lord! I seek refuge with Thee from the suggestions of the Evil Ones. And I seek refuge with Thee O my Lord! Lest they should come near me." (23:97-98)

Those who dispute about the signs of Allah without any authority bestowed on them, there is nothing in their breasts but (the quest of) greatness, which they shall never attain to: seek refuge, then, in Allah: It is He Who hears and sees (all things). (40:56)

And if (at any time) an incitement to discord is made to thee by the Evil One, seek refuge in Allah. He is the One Who hears and knows all things. (41:36)

Say: I seek refuge with the Lord of the Dawn. (113:1)

Say: I seek refuge with the Lord and Cherisher of Mankind. (114:1)

Seek Sustenance From Him

And remember We took a covenant from the Children of Israel (to this effect): Worship none but Allah; treat with kindness your parents and kindred, and orphans and those in need; speak fair to the people; be steadfast in prayer; and practice regular charity. Then did ye turn back, except a few among you, and ye backslide (even now). (2:83)

O you who believe, violate not the signs of Allah, nor the Sacred Month, nor the offerings, nor the victims with garlands, nor those repairing to the Sacred House seeking the grace and pleasure of their Lord. And when you are free from pilgrimage obligations, then hunt. And let not hatred of a people - because they hindered you from the Sacred Mosque - incite you to transgress. And help one another in righteousness and piety, and help not one another in sin and aggression, and keep your duty to Allah. Surely Allah is severe in requiting (evil). (5:2)

And certainly Allah made a covenant with the Children of Israel, and We raised up among them twelve chieftains. And Allah said: Surely I am with you. If you keep up prayer and pay the poor-rate and believe in My messengers and assist them and offer to Allah a goodly gift, I will certainly cover your evil deeds, and cause you to enter Gardens wherein rivers flow. But whoever among you disbelieves after that, he indeed strays from the right way. (5:12)

And with those who say, We are Christians, We made a covenant, but they neglected a portion of that whereof they were reminded so We stirred up enmity and hatred among them to the day of Resurrection. And Allah will soon inform them of what they did. (5:14)

Whereby Allah guides such as follow His pleasure into the ways of peace, and brings them out of darkness into light by His will, and guides them to the right path. (5:16)

And if they had observed the Torah and the Gospel and that which is revealed to them from their Lord, they would certainly have eaten from above them and from beneath their feet. There is a party of them keeping to the moderate course; and most of them - evil is that which they do. (5:66)

And out of His mercy He has made for you the night and the day, that you may rest therein, and that you may seek of His grace, and that you may give thanks. (28:73)

You only worship idols besides Allah and you invent a lie. Surely they whom you serve besides Allah control no sustenance for you; so seek sustenance from Allah and serve Him and be grateful to Him. To Him you will be brought back. (29:17)

But when the prayer is ended, disperse abroad in the land and seek of Allah's grace, and remember Allah much, that you may be successful. (62:10)

Shapes You In The Wombs

Who shapes you in the wombs as He pleases. There is no god but Exalted in Might, the Wise. (3:6)

created you from a single being, then made its mates of the same And He sent down for you eight of the cattle in pairs. He creates the wombs of your mothers - creation after creation - in triple s. That is Allah, your Lord; His is the kingdom. There is no God How are you then turned away? (39:6)

Takes Account Of Every Single Thing

h belongeth all that is in the heavens and on earth. Whether ye hat is in your minds or conceal it, Allah Calleth you to account e forgiveth whom He pleaseth, and punisheth whom He pleaseth, h hath power over all things. (2:284)

may know that they have truly delivered the messages of their nd He encompasses what is with them, and He keeps account of s. (72:28)

The Heavens And Earth Belong To Allah

h belongeth all that is in the heavens and on earth. Whether ye hat is in your minds or conceal it, Allah Calleth you to account e forgiveth whom He pleaseth, and punisheth whom He pleaseth, h hath power over all things. (2:284)

h belongs all that is in the heavens and on earth: To Him do all ns go back (for decision). (3:109)

h belongeth all that is in the heavens and on earth. He forgiveth He pleaseth and punisheth whom He pleaseth; but Allah is Oft-ng, Most Merciful. (3:129)

Allah belong all things in the heavens and on earth: And He it is compasseth all things. (4:126)

What Is With Allah Will Endure

What is with you must vanish: what is with Allah will endure. And We will certainly bestow, on those who patiently persevere, their reward according to the best of their actions. (16:96)

The (material) things which ye are given are but the conveniences of this life and the glitter thereof; but that which is with Allah is better and more enduring: will ye not then be wise? (28:60)

So whatever you are given is but a provision of this world's life, and that which Allah has is better and more lasting for those who believe and rely on their Lord. (42:36)

Allah Will Change Evil Into Good

Except him who repents and believes and does good deeds; for such Allah changes their evil deeds to good ones. And Allah is ever Forgiving, Merciful. (25:70)

Allah Will Change The Condition Of A People

For each (such person) there are (angels) in succession, before and behind him: They guard him by command of Allah. Allah does not change a people's lot unless they change what is in their hearts. But when (once) Allah willeth a people's punishment, there can be no turning it back, nor will they find, besides Him, any to protect. (13:11)

Allah Will Not Suffer Your Reward To Be Lost

And their Lord hath accepted of them, and answered them: "Never will I suffer to be lost the work of any of you, be he male or female: Ye are members, one of another: Those who have left their homes, or been driven out therefrom, or suffered harm in My Cause, or fought or been slain, verily, I will blot out from them their iniquities, and admit them into Gardens with rivers flowing beneath;- A reward from the presence of Allah, and from His presence is the best of rewards." (3:195)

It was not fitting for the people of Medina and the Bedouin Arabs of the neighbourhood, to refuse to follow Allah's Messenger, nor to prefer their own lives to his: because nothing could they suffer or do, but was reckoned to their credit as a deed of righteousness, whether they suffered thirst, or fatigue, or hunger, in the cause of Allah, or trod paths to raise the ire of the Unbelievers, or received any injury whatever from an enemy: for Allah suffereth not the reward to be lost of those who do good. (9:20)

As to those who believe and work righteousness, verily We shall not suffer to perish the reward of any who do a (single) righteous deed. (18:30)

As to those who believe and work righteousness, verily We shall not suffer to perish the reward of any who do a (single) righteous deed. (21:94)

And those who believe and whose offspring follow them in faith - We unite with them their off-spring and We shall deprive them of naught of their work. Every man is pledged for what he does. (52:21)

Meeting With Your Lord

Who bear in mind the certainty that they are to meet their Lord, and that they are to return to Him. (2:46)

Your wives are as a tilth unto you; so approach your tilth when or how ye will; but do some good act for your souls beforehand; and fear Allah. And know that ye are to meet Him (in the Hereafter), and give (these) good tidings to those who believe. (2:223)

When Talut set forth with the armies, he said: "Allah will test you at the stream: if any drinks of its water, He goes not with my army: Only those who taste not of it go with me: A mere sip out of the hand is excused." but they all drank of it, except a few. When they crossed the river, He and the faithful ones with him, they said: "This day We cannot cope with Goliath and his forces." But those who were convinced that they must meet Allah, said: "How oft, by Allah's will, Hath a small force vanquished a big one? Allah is with those who steadfastly persevere." (2:249)

Moreover, We gave Moses the Book, completing (Our favour) to those who would do right, and explaining all things in detail, and a guide and a mercy, that they might believe in the meeting with their Lord. (6:154)

If Allah were to hasten for men the ill (they have earned) as they would fain hasten on the good, then would their respite be settled at once. But We leave those who rest not their hope on their meeting with Us, in their trespasses, wandering in distraction to and fro. (10:11)

One day He will gather them together: (It will be) as if they had tarried but an hour of a day: they will recognize each other: assuredly those will be lost who denied the meeting with Allah and refused to receive true guidance. (10:45)

Allah is He Who raised the heavens without any pillars that ye can see; is firmly established on the throne (of authority); He has subjected the sun and the moon (to his Law)! Each one runs (its course) for a term appointed. He doth regulate all affairs, explaining the signs in detail, that ye may believe with certainty in the meeting with your Lord. (13:2)

And they will be marshalled before thy Lord in ranks, (with the announcement), "Now have ye come to Us (bare) as We created you first: aye, ye thought We shall not fulfill the appointment made to you to meet (Us)!" (18:48)

Say: "I am but a man like yourselves, (but) the inspiration has come to me, that your Allah is one Allah: whoever expects to meet his Lord, let him work righteousness, and, in the worship of his Lord, admit no one as partner. (18:110)

Such as fear not the meeting with Us (for Judgment) say: "Why are not the angels sent down to us, or (why) do we not see our Lord?" Indeed they have an arrogant conceit of themselves, and mighty is the insolence of their impiety! (25:21)

For those whose hopes are in the meeting with Allah (in the Hereafter, let them strive); for the term (appointed) by Allah is surely coming and He hears and knows (all things). (29:5)

Those who reject the Signs of Allah and the Meeting with Him (in the Hereafter), it is they who shall despair of My Mercy: it is they who will (suffer) a most grievous Penalty. (29:23)

Do they not reflect in their own minds? Not but for just ends and for a term appointed, did Allah create the heavens and the earth, and all between them: yet are there truly many among men who deny the meeting with their Lord (at the Resurrection)! (30:8)

And they say: "What! When we lie, hidden and lost, in the earth, shall we indeed be in a Creation renewed? Nay, they deny the Meeting with their Lord." (32:10)

"Taste ye then - for ye forgot the Meeting of this Day of yours, and We too will forget you - taste ye the Penalty of Eternity for your (evil) deeds!" (32:14)

Their salutation on the Day they meet Him will be "Peace!" And He has prepared for them a generous Reward. (33:44)

Ah indeed! Are they in doubt concerning the Meeting with their Lord? Ah indeed! It is He that doth encompass all things! (41:54)

O thou man! Verily thou art ever toiling on towards thy Lord- painfully toiling, but thou shalt meet Him. (84:6)

Nearness to Him

When My servants ask thee concerning Me, I am indeed close (to them): I listen to the prayer of every suppliant when he calleth on Me: Let them also, with a will, Listen to My call, and believe in Me: That they may walk in the right way. (2:186)

Say: Shall I give you glad tidings of things far better than those? For the righteous are Gardens in nearness to their Lord, with rivers flowing beneath; therein is their eternal home; with companions pure (and holy); and the good pleasure of Allah. For in Allah's sight are (all) His servants. (3:15)

Those who are near to thy Lord, disdain not to do Him worship: They celebrate His praises, and prostrate before Him. (7:206)

To the Thamud People (We sent) Salih, one of their own brethren. He said: "O my people! Worship Allah: ye have no other god but Him. It is He Who hath produced you from the earth and settled you therein: then ask forgiveness of Him, and turn to Him (in repentance): for my Lord is (always) near, ready to answer." (11:61)

It is not your wealth nor your sons, that will bring you nearer to Us in degree: but only those who believe and work righteousness - these are the ones for whom there is a multiplied Reward for their deeds, while secure they (reside) in the dwellings on high! (34:37)

Say: "If I am astray, I only stray to the loss of my own soul: but if I receive guidance, it is because of the inspiration of my Lord to me: it is He Who hears all things, and is (ever) near." (34:50)

So We forgave him this (lapse): he enjoyed, indeed, a Near Approach to Us, and a beautiful place of (Final) Return. (38:25)

And he enjoyed, indeed, a Near Approach to Us, and a beautiful Place of (Final) Return. (38:40)

Is it not to Allah that sincere devotion is due? But those who take for protectors other than Allah (say): "We only serve them in order that they may bring us nearer to Allah." Truly Allah will judge between them in that wherein they differ. But Allah guides not such as are false and ungrateful. (39:3)

It was We Who created man, and We know what dark suggestions his soul makes to him: for We are nearer to him than (his) jugular vein. (50:16)

And you are three sorts. So those on the right hand; how (happy) are those on the right-hand! And those on the left; how (wretched) are those on the left! And the foremost are the foremost - These are drawn nigh (to

In Gardens of bliss a multitude from among the first, and a few among those of later times, on thrones inwrought, reclining on facing each other. Round about them will go youths never altering with goblets and ewers, and a cup of pure drink. They are not with headache thereby, nor are they intoxicated, and fruits that loose, and flesh of fowl that they desire, and pure, beautiful ones, hidden pearls. A reward for what they did. They hear therein no sinful talk - but only the saying, Peace! Peace! And those on the hand; how (happy) are those on the right hand! Amid thornless lote-and clustered banana-trees, and extensive shade, and water and abundant fruit, neither intercepted, nor forbidden. (56:7-33)

Allah sets forth, as an example to those who believe the wife of Behold she said: "O my Lord! Build for me, in nearness to mansion in the Garden, and save me from Pharaoh and his and save me from those that do wrong." (66:11)

BELIEVERS

Allah Has Purchased The Believers

Surely Allah has bought from the believers their persons and their property - theirs (in return) is the Garden. They fight in Allah's way, so they slay and are slain. It is a promise which is binding on Him in the Torah and the Gospel and the Qur'an. And who is more faithful to his promise than Allah? Rejoice therefore in your bargain which you have made. And that is the mighty achievement. (9:111)

Allah Is With The Believers

(O Unbelievers!) If ye prayed for victory and judgment, now hath the judgment come to you: if ye desist (from wrong), it will be best for you: if ye return (to the attack), so shall We. Not the least good will your forces be to you even if they were multiplied: for verily Allah is with those who believe! (8:19)

And be not slack so as to cry for peace - and you are the uppermost - and Allah is with you, and He will not bring your deeds to naught. (47:35)

Allah Listens To The Believers

And He listens to those who believe and do deeds of righteousness, and gives them increase of His Bounty: but for the Unbelievers their is a terrible Penalty. (42:26)

Allah Puts Affection In The Believers' Hearts

And (moreover) He hath put affection between their hearts: not if thou hadst spent all that is in the earth, couldst thou have produced that affection, but Allah hath done it: for He is Exalted in might, Wise. (8:63)

Believers Are The Best Of Creatures

Those who believe and do good, they are the best of creatures. (98:7)

Believers Are A Single Brotherhood

The Believers are but a single Brotherhood: So make peace and reconciliation between your two (contending) brothers; and fear Allah, that ye may receive Mercy. (49:10)

The Believers Description

The Messenger believes in what has been revealed to him from his Lord, and (so do) the believers. They all believe in Allah and His angels and His Books and His messengers. We make no difference between any of His messengers. And they say: We hear and obey; our Lord, Thy forgiveness (do we crave), and to Thee is the eventual course. (2:285)

For, Believers are those who, when Allah is mentioned, feel a tremor in their hearts, and when they hear His signs rehearsed, find their faith strengthened, and put (all) their trust in their Lord; Who establish regular prayers and spend (freely) out of the gifts We have given them for sustenance: Such in truth are the believers: they have grades of dignity with their Lord, and forgiveness, and generous sustenance. (8:2-4)

Those who believe, and adopt exile, and fight for the Faith, in the cause of Allah as well as those who give (them) asylum and aid, these are (all) in very truth the Believers: for them is the forgiveness of sins and a provision most generous. (8:74)

They who turn (to Allah), who serve (Him), who praise (Him), who fast, who bow down, who prostrate themselves, who enjoin what is good and forbid what is evil, and who keep the limits of Allah - and give good news to the believers. (9:112)

Seest thou not that Allah created the heavens and the earth with truth? If He please, He will take you away and bring a new creation, and that is not difficult for Allah. And those who join that which Allah has bidden to be joined and have awe of their Lord, and fear the evil reckoning. And those who are steadfast seeking the pleasure of their Lord, and keep up prayer and spend of that which We have given them, secretly and openly, and repel evil with good; for such is the (happy) issue of the abode. (13:19-22)

Those who believe and whose hearts find rest in the remembrance of Allah. Now surely in Allah's remembrance do hearts find rest. Those who believe and do good, a good final state is theirs and a goodly return. (13:28-29)

In the name of Allah, the Beneficent, the Merciful. Successful indeed are the believers, Who are humble in their prayers, And who shun what is vain, And who act for the sake of purity, And who restrain their sexual passions - except in the presence of their mates or those whom their right hands possess, for such surely are not blamable. But whoever seeks to go beyond that, such are transgressors. And those who are keepers of their trusts and their covenant, and those who keep a guard on their prayers. these are the heirs, who inherit Paradise. Therein they will abide. (23:1-11)

The response of the believers, when they are invited to Allah and His Messenger that He may judge between them, is only that they say: We hear and we obey. And these it is that are successful. (24:51)

Only those are believers who believe in Allah and his Messenger, and when they are with him on a momentous affair, they go not away until they have asked leave of him. Surely they who ask leave of thee, are they who believe in Allah and His Messenger; so when they ask leave of thee for some affair of theirs, give leave to whom thou wilt of them, and ask forgiveness for them from Allah. Surely Allah is Forgiving, Merciful. (24:62)

A guidance and good news for the believers, Who keep up prayer and pay the poor-rate, and they are sure of the Hereafter. (24:2-3)

Only they believe in Our messages who, when they are reminded of them, fall down prostrate and celebrate the praise of their Lord, and they are not proud. They forsake (their) beds, calling upon their Lord in fear and in hope, and spend out of what We have given them. So no soul knows what refreshment of the eyes is hidden for them: a reward for what they did. Is he then, who is a believer, like him who is a transgressor? They are not equal. As for those who believe and do good deeds, for them are Gardens, a refuge - an entertainment for what they did. (32:15-19)

This because those who reject Allah follow vanities, while those who believe follow the Truth from their Lord: Thus does Allah set forth for men their lessons by similitudes. (47:3)

Muhammad is the Messenger of Allah, and those with him are firm of heart against the disbelievers, compassionate among themselves. Thou seest them blowing down, prostrating themselves, seeking Allah's grace and pleasure. Their marks are on their faces in consequence of prostration. That is their description in the Torah - and their description in the Gospel - like seed-produce that puts forth its sprout, then strengthens it, so it becomes stout and stands firmly on its stem, delighting the sowers that He may enrage the disbelievers on account of them. Allah has promised such of them as believe and do good, forgiveness and a great reward. (48:29)

The believers are those only who believe in Allah and His Messenger, then they doubt not, and struggle hard with their wealth and their lives in the way of Allah. Such are the truthful ones. (49:15)

Thou wilt not find a people who believe in Allah and the latter day loving those who oppose Allah and His Messenger, even though they be their fathers, or their sons, or their brothers, or their kinsfolk. These are they into whose hearts He has impressed faith, and strengthened them with a Spirit from Himself, and He will cause them to enter Gardens wherein flow rivers, abiding therein. Allah is well-pleased with them and they are well-pleased with Him. These are Allah's party. Now surely it is Allah's party who are the successful! (58:22)

Except those who pray, Who are constant at their prayer, and in whose wealth there is a known right for the beggar and the destitute, and those who accept the truth of the day of Judgment: and those who are fearful of the chastisement of their Lord - surely the chastisement of their Lord is (a thing) not to be felt secure from - and those who restrain their sexual passions, except in the presence of their mates or those whom their right hands possess - for such surely are not to be blamed, but he who seeks to go beyond this, these are the transgressors. And those who are faithful to their trusts and their covenant, and those who are upright in their testimonies, and those who keep a guard on their prayer. These are in Gardens, honoured. (70:22-35)

Then he is of those who believe and exhort one another to patience, and exhort one another to mercy. (90:17)

Except those who believe and do good, and exhort one another to Truth, and exhort one another to patience. (103:3)

Sin To Annoy Believers

And those who annoy believing men and believing women undeservedly, they bear the guilt of slander and manifest sin. (33:58)

Don't Disrespect Believers

O you who believe, let not people laugh at people, perchance they may be better than they; nor let women (laugh) at women, perchance they may be better than they. Neither find fault with your own people, nor call one another by nicknames. Evil is a bad name after faith; and whoso turns not, these it is that are the iniquitous. O you who believe, avoid most of suspicion, for surely suspicion in some cases is sin; and spy not nor let some of you backbite others. Does one of you like to eat the flesh of his dead brother? You abhor it! And keep your duty to Allah, surely Allah is Oft-returning (to mercy), Merciful. (49:11-12)

Honor Belongs To The Believers

They say, "If we return to Medina, surely the more honourable (element) will expel therefrom the meaner." But honour belongs to Allah and His Messenger, and to the Believers; but the Hypocrites know not. (63:8)

Allah Loves The Believers

Those who believe and do good deeds, for them the Beneficent will surely bring about love. (19:96)

...ng **Men and Women**

...e believers, men and women, are friends one of another. They
...good and forbid evil and keep up prayer and pay the poor-rate,
...y Allah and His Messenger. As for these, Allah will have mercy
...n. Surely Allah is Mighty, Wise. Allah has promised to the
...rs, men and women, Gardens, wherein flow rivers, to abide
...and goodly dwellings in Gardens of perpetual abode. And
...of all is Allah's goodly pleasure. That is the grand achievement.
...2)

...the men who submit and the women who submit, and the
...ng men and the believing women, and the truthful men and the
...women, and the patient men and the patient women, and the
...men and the humble women, and the charitable men and the
...le women, and the fasting men and the fasting women, and the
...o guard their chastity and the women who guard, and the men
...member Allah much and the women who remember - Allah has
...d for them forgiveness and a mighty reward. (33:35)

...rs **Shall Not Fear Nor Grieve**

...d: "Get ye down all from here; and if, as is sure, there comes to
...idance from me, whosoever follows My guidance, on them shall
...ar, nor shall they grieve. (2:38)
...those who believe, and those who are Jews, and the Christians,
...Sabians, whoever believes in Allah and the Last Day and does
...hey have their reward with their Lord, and there is no fear for
...or shall they grieve. (2:62)

...hoever submits himself entirely to Allah and he is the doer of
...others), he has his reward from his Lord, and there is no fear for
...r shall they grieve. (2:112)

...who spend their wealth in the way of Allah, then follow not up
...ey have spent with reproach or injury, their reward is with their
...nd they shall have no fear nor shall they grieve. (2:262)

Those who (in charity) spend of their goods by night and by day, in secret and in public, have their reward with their Lord: on them shall be no fear, nor shall they grieve. (2:274)

Those who believe and do good deeds and keep up prayer and pay the poor-rate - their reward is with their Lord; and they have no fear, nor shall they grieve. (2:277)

Allah will blot out usury, and He causes charity to prosper. And Allah loves not any ungrateful sinner. (3:170)

Surely those who believe and those who are Jews and the Sabians and the Christians - whoever believes in Allah and the Last Day and does good - they shall have no fear nor shall they grieve. (5:69)

And We send not messengers but as bearers of good news and warners; then whoever believes and acts aright, they shall have no fear, nor shall they grieve. (6:48)

O children of Adam, if messengers come to you from among you relating to you My messages, then whosoever guards against evil and acts aright - they shall have no fear, nor shall they grieve. (7:35)

Now surely the friends of Allah, they have no fear nor do they grieve. (10:62)

But Allah will deliver the righteous to their place of salvation: no evil shall touch them, nor shall they grieve. (39:61)

Surely those who say, Our Lord is Allah, then continue on the right way, on them is no fear, nor shall they grieve. (46:13)

Believers Have Strong Love For Allah

Yet there are some men who take for themselves objects of worship besides Allah, whom they love as they should love Allah. And those who believe are stronger in (their) love for Allah. And O that the wrongdoers had seen, when they see the chastisement, that power is wholly Allah's, and that Allah is severe in chastising! (2:165)

Believers Are Protectors Of One Another

Surely those who believed and fled (their homes) and struggled hard in Allah's way with their wealth and their lives, and those who gave shelter and helped - these are friends one of another. And those who believed and did not flee, you are not responsible for their protection until they flee. And if they seek help from you in the matter of religion, it is your duty to help (them) except against a people between whom and you there is a treaty. And Allah is Seer of what you do. (8:72)

The Believers, men and women, are protectors one of another: they enjoin what is just, and forbid what is evil: they observe regular prayers, practice regular charity, and obey Allah and His Messenger. On them will Allah pour His mercy: for Allah is Exalted in power, Wise. (9:71)

And those who, when an oppressive wrong is inflicted on them, (are not cowed but) help and defend themselves. (42:39)

Believers Are Rewarded

Those who believe, and do deeds of righteousness, and establish regular prayers and regular charity, will have their reward with their Lord: on them shall be no fear, nor shall they grieve. (2:277)

Verily this Qur'an doth guide to that which is most right (or stable), and giveth the Glad Tidings to the Believers who work deeds of righteousness, that they shall have a magnificent reward. (17:9)

Rightly directing, to give warning of severe punishment from Him and to give good news to the believers who do good that theirs is a goodly reward, Staying in it forever. (18:2-3)

These are the heirs, Who inherit Paradise. Therein they will abide. (23:10-11)

So no soul knows what refreshment of the eyes is hidden for them: a reward for what they did. (32:17)

Their salutation on the Day they meet Him will be "Peace!" And He has prepared for them a generous Reward. (33:44)

Then give the Glad Tidings to the Believers, that they shall have from Allah a very great Bounty. (33:47)

That He may reward those who believe and do good. For them is forgiveness and an honourable sustenance. (34:4)

And it is not your wealth, nor your children, that bring you near to Us in rank; but whoever believes and does good, for such is a double reward for what they do, and they are secure in the highest places. (34:37)

Those who believe and do good, for them is surely a reward never to be cut off. (41:8)

Then as to those who believed and did good, their Lord will admit them to His mercy. That is the manifest achievement. (45:30)

Muhammad is the Messenger of Allah, and those with him are firm of heart against the disbelievers, compassionate among themselves. Thou seest them bowing down, prostrating themselves, seeking Allah's grace and pleasure. Their marks are on their faces in consequence of prostration. That is their description in the Torah - and their description in the Gospel - like seed-produce that puts forth its sprout, then strengthens it, so it becomes stout and stands firmly on its stem, delighting the sowers that He may enrage the disbelievers on account of them. Allah has promised such of them as believe and do good, forgiveness and a great reward. (48:29)

Believe in Allah and His Messenger, and spend of that whereof He has made you heirs. So those of you who believe and spend - for them is a great reward. (57:7)

And those who believe in Allah and His messengers - they are the Sincere (lovers of Truth), and the witnesses (who testify), in the eyes of their Lord: They shall have their Reward and their Light. But those who reject Allah and deny Our Signs, they are the Companions of Hell-Fire. (57:19)

Except to those who believe and work righteous deeds: For them is a Reward that will never fail. (84:25)

Except such as believe and do righteous deeds: For they shall have a reward unfailing. (95:6)

Believers Will Be Rewarded With A Garden

But give glad tidings to those who believe and work righteousness, that their portion is Gardens, beneath which rivers flow. Every time they are fed with fruits therefrom, they say: "Why, this is what we were fed with before," for they are given things in similitude; and they have therein companions pure (and holy); and they abide therein (forever). (2:25)

Allah hath promised to Believers, men and women, gardens under which rivers flow, to dwell therein, and beautiful mansions in gardens of everlasting bliss. But the greatest bliss is the good pleasure of Allah: that is the supreme felicity. (9:72)

And those who are steadfast seeking the pleasure of their Lord, and keep up prayer and spend of that which We have given them, secretly and openly, and repel evil with good; for such is the (happy) issue of the abode - Garden of perpetuity, which they will enter along with those who do good from among their fathers and their spouses and their offspring; and the angels will enter in upon them from every gate. Peace be to you, because you were constant - how excellent is then the final Abode! (13:22-24)

But those who believe and work righteousness will be admitted to gardens beneath which rivers flow, to dwell therein for aye with the leave of their Lord. Their greeting therein will be: "Peace!" (14:23)

Except those who repent and believe and do good - such will enter the Garden, and they will not be wronged in aught: Gardens of perpetuity which the Beneficent has promised to His servants in the Unseen. Surely His promise ever comes to pass. They will hear therein no vain discourse, but only, Peace! And they have their sustenance therein, morning and evening. This is the Garden which We cause those of Our servants to inherit who keep their duty. (19:60-63)

And whoso comes to Him a believer, having done good deeds, for them are high ranks - Gardens of perpetuity, wherein flow rivers, to abide therein. And such is the reward of him who purifies himself. (20:75-76)

Allah will admit those who believe and work righteous deeds, to Gardens beneath which rivers flow: they shall be adorned therein with bracelets of gold and pearls; and their garments there will be of silk. (22:23)

For those who believe and do righteous deeds are Gardens as hospitable homes, for their (good) deeds. (32:19)

Thou seest the unjust fearing on account of what they have earned, and it must befall them. And those who believe and do good are in the meadows of the Gardens - they have what they please with their Lord. That is the great grace. (42:22)

O My servants, there is no fear for you this day, nor will you grieve - Those who believed in Our messages and submitted (to Us), Enter the Garden, you and your wives, being made happy. Sent round to them are golden bowls and drinking-cups, and therein is that which (their) souls yearn for and the eyes delight in, and therein you will abide. And this is the Garden, which you are made to inherit on account of what you did. For you therein is abundant fruit to eat thereof. (43:68-73)

Verily Allah will admit those who believe and do righteous deeds, to Gardens beneath which rivers flow; while those who reject Allah will enjoy (this world) and eat as cattle eat; and the Fire will be their abode. (47:12)

That He may cause the believing men and the believing women to enter Gardens wherein flow rivers to abide therein and remove from them their evil. And that is a grand achievement with Allah. (48:5)

On that day thou wilt see the faithful men and the faithful women, their light gleaming before them and on their right hand. Good news for you this day! Gardens wherein rivers flow, to abide therein! That is the grand achievement. (57:12)

lt not find a people who believe in Allah and the latter day loving
ho oppose Allah and His Messenger, even though they be their
or their sons, or their brothers, or their kinsfolk. These are they
ose hearts He has impressed faith, and strengthened them with a
from Himself, and He will cause them to enter Gardens wherein
ers, abiding therein. Allah is well-pleased with them and they are
ased with Him. These are Allah's party. Now surely it is Allah's
ho are the successful! (58:22)

forgive you your sins, and admit you to Gardens beneath which
flow, and to beautiful mansions in Gardens of Eternity: that is
the Supreme Achievement. (61:12)

when He will gather you for the day of Gathering, that is the day
Manifestation of losses. And whoever believes in Allah and does
e will remove from him his evil and cause him to enter Gardens
rivers flow, to abide therein for ever. That is the great
ment. (64:9)

enger who recites to you the clear messages of Allah so that he
ng forth those who believe and do good deeds from darkness into
nd whoever believes in Allah and does good deeds, He will cause
enter Gardens wherein rivers flow, to abide therein for ever. Allah
ed given him a goodly sustenance. (65:11)

ho believe! Turn to Allah with sincere repentance: In the hope
r Lord will remove from you your ills and admit you to Gardens
which Rivers flow the Day that Allah will not permit to be
ted the Prophet and those who believe with him. Their Light will
ward before them and by their right hands, while they say, "Our
Perfect our Light for us, and grant us Forgiveness: for Thou hast
ver all things." (66:8)

ll be the honoured ones in the Gardens (of Bliss). (70:35)

who believe and do good, theirs are Gardens wherein flow rivers.
the great achievement. (85:11)

Their reward is with their Lord: Gardens of perpetuity wherein flow rivers, abiding therein for ever. Allah is well pleased with them and they are well pleased with Him. That is for him who fears his Lord. (98:8)

Why Say That Which You Do Not

O ye who believe! Why say ye that which ye do not? (61:2)

DELIVERANCE

Then We deliver Our messengers and those who believe - even so (now); it is binding on Us to deliver the believers. (10:103)

So judge Thou between me and them openly, and deliver me and the believers who are with me. So We delivered him and those with him in the laden ark. (26:118-119)

And We delivered those who believed and kept their duty. (27:53)

But We delivered those who believed and practiced righteousness. (41:18)

Then We evacuated those of the Believers who were there, But We found not there any just (Muslim) persons except in one house. (51:35-36)

Rejoicing because of what their Lord has given them; and their Lord saved them from the chastisement of the burning Fire. (52:18)

"But Allah has been good to us, and has delivered us from the Penalty of the Scorching Wind. (52:27)

But Allah will deliver them from the evil of that Day, and will shed over them a Light of Beauty and (blissful) Joy. (76:11)

Allah Turns Mercifully To The Believers

That Allah may chastise the hypocritical men and the hypocritical women and the polytheistic men and the polytheistic women, and Allah will turn (mercifully) to the believing men and the believing women. And Allah is ever Forgiving, Merciful. (33:73)

Allah Will Remove The Ills And Improve The Condition Of The Believers

So their Lord accepted their prayer, (saying): I will not suffer the work of any worker among you to be lost whether male or female, the one of you being the other. So those who fled and were driven forth from their homes and persecuted in My way and who fought and were slain, I shall truly remove their evil and make them enter Gardens wherein flow rivers - a reward from Allah. And with Allah is the best reward. (3:195)

And those who believe and do good, and believe in that which has been revealed to Muhammad - and it is the Truth from their Lord - He will remove their evil from them and improve their condition. (47:2)

That He may cause the believing men and the believing women to enter Gardens wherein flow rivers to abide therein and remove from them their evil. And that is a grand achievement with Allah. (48:5)

The day when He will gather you for the day of Gathering, that is the day of the Manifestation of losses. And whoever believes in Allah and does good, he will remove from him his evil and cause him to enter Gardens wherein rivers flow, to abide therein for ever. That is the great achievement. (64:9)

Forgives Sins

To Allah belongs whatever is in the heavens and whatever is in the earth. And whether you manifest what is in your minds or hide it, Allah will call you to account according to it. So he forgives whom He pleases and chastises whom He pleases. And Allah is Possessor of power over all things. (2:284)

Say: "If ye do love Allah, Follow me: Allah will love you and forgive you your sins: For Allah is Oft-Forgiving, Most Merciful." (3:31)

And their Lord hath accepted of them, and answered them: "Never will I suffer to be lost the work of any of you, be he male or female: Ye are members, one of another: Those who have left their homes, or been driven out therefrom, or suffered harm in My Cause, or fought or been slain,- verily, I will blot out from them their iniquities, and admit them into Gardens with rivers flowing beneath;- A reward from the presence of Allah, and from His presence is the best of rewards." (3:195)

Allah forgiveth not that partners should be set up with Him; but He forgiveth anything else, to whom He pleaseth; to set up partners with Allah is to devise a sin most heinous indeed. (4:48)

Allah forgiveth not (the sin of) joining other gods with Him; but He forgiveth whom He pleaseth other sins than this: one who joins other gods with Allah, Hath strayed far, far away (from the right). (4:116)

But if the thief repents after his crime, and amends his conduct, Allah turneth to him in forgiveness; for Allah is Oft-forgiving, Most Merciful. Knowest thou not that to Allah (alone) belongeth the dominion of the heavens and the earth? He punisheth whom He pleaseth, and He forgiveth whom He pleaseth: and Allah hath power over all things. (5:39-40)

And remember it was said to them: "Dwell in this town and eat therein as ye wish, but say the word of humility and enter the gate in a posture of humility: We shall forgive you your faults; We shall increase (the portion of) those who do good." (7:161)

O you who believe, if you keep your duty to Allah, He will grant you a distinction and do away with your evils and protect you. And Allah is the Lord of mighty grace. (8:29)

O Prophet, say to those of the captives who are in your hands: If Allah knows anything good in your hearts, He will give you better than that which has been taken from you, and will forgive you. And Allah is Forgiving, Merciful. (8:70)

He said: "This day let no reproach be (cast) on you: Allah will forgive you, and He is the Most Merciful of those who show mercy!" (12:92)

They ask thee to hasten on the evil in preference to the good: Yet have come to pass, before them, (many) exemplary punishments! But verily thy Lord is full of forgiveness for mankind for their wrong-doing, and verily thy Lord is (also) strict in punishment. (13:6)

Their messengers said: "Is there a doubt about Allah, The Creator of the heavens and the earth? It is He Who invites you, in order that He may forgive you your sins and give you respite for a term appointed!" They said: "Ah! Ye are no more than human, like ourselves! Ye wish to turn us away from the (gods) our fathers used to worship: then bring us some clear authority." (14:10)

He prayed: "O my Lord! I have indeed wronged my soul! Do Thou then forgive me!" So (Allah) forgave him: for He is the Oft-Forgiving, Most Merciful. (28:16)

That He may make your conduct whole and sound and forgive you your sins: He that obeys Allah and His Messenger, has already attained the highest achievement. (33:71)

"For that my Lord has granted me Forgiveness and has enrolled me among those held in honour!" (36:27)

Say: O My servants who have been prodigal regarding their souls, despair not of the mercy of Allah; surely Allah forgives sins altogether. He is indeed the Forgiving, the Merciful. (39:53)

Who forgiveth sin, accepteth repentance, is strict in punishment, and hath a long reach (in all things). There is no god but He: to Him is the final goal. (40:3)

And He it is Who accepts repentance from his servants and pardons evil deeds, and He knows what you do. (42:25)

Whatever misfortune happens to you, is because on the things your hands have wrought, and for many (of them) He grants forgiveness. (42:30)

Or He can cause them to perish because of the (evil) which (the men) have earned; but much doth He forgive. (42:34)

O our people, accept the Inviter to Allah and believe in Him. He will forgive you some of your sins and protect you from a painful chastisement. (46:31)

h belongs the dominion of the heavens and the earth: He forgives He wills, and He punishes whom He wills: but Allah is Oft-ng, Most Merciful. (48:14)

who believe, keep your duty to Allah and believe in His ger - He will give you two portions of His mercy, and give you a which you shall walk, and forgive you. And Allah is Forgiving, ul. (57:28)

fear that you will not (be able to) give in charity before your ation? So when you do not do it and Allah has turned to you ully), then keep up prayer and pay the poor-rate and obey Allah Messenger; and Allah is Aware of what you do. (58:13)

forgive you your sins, and admit you to Gardens beneath which flow, and to beautiful mansions in Gardens of Eternity: that is the Supreme Achievement. (61:12)

et apart for Allah a goodly portion, He will double it for you and you. And Allah is the multiplier (of rewards), Forbearing. (64:17)

may forgive you your sins and give you respite for a stated Term: n the Term given by Allah is accomplished, it cannot be put l: if ye only knew." (71:4)

PATIENCE (SABUR)

And seek assistance through patience and prayer, and this is hard except for the humble ones. (2:45)

O ye who believe! Seek help with patient perseverance and prayer; for Allah is with those who patiently persevere. (2:153)

It is not righteousness that you turn your faces towards the East and the West, but righteous is the one who believes in Allah, and the Last Day, and the angels and the Book and the prophets, and gives away wealth out of love for Him to the near of kin and the orphans and the needy and the wayfarer and to those who ask and to set slaves free and keeps up prayer and pays the poor-rate; and the performers of their promise when they make a promise, and the patient in distress and affliction and in the time of conflict. These are they who are truthful; and these are they who keep their duty. (2:177)

Those who show patience, firmness and self-control; who are true (in word and deed); who worship devoutly; who spend (in the way of Allah); and who pray for forgiveness in the early hours of the morning. (3:17)

Ye shall certainly be tried and tested in your possessions and in your personal selves; and ye shall certainly hear much that will grieve you, from those who received the Book before you and from those who worship many gods. But if ye persevere patiently, and guard against evil, then that will be a determining factor in all affairs. (3:186)

O ye who believe! Persevere in patience and constancy; vie in such perseverance; strengthen each other; and fear Allah; that ye may prosper. (3:200)

Rejected were the messengers before thee: with patience and constancy they bore their rejection and their wrongs, until Our aid did reach them: there is none that can alter the words (and decrees) of Allah. Already hast thou received some account of those messengers. (6:34)

And if there is a party among you who believes in the message with which I have been sent, and a party which does not believe, hold yourselves in patience until Allah doth decide between us: for He is the best to decide. (7:87)

But thou dost wreak thy vengeance on us simply because we believed in the Signs of our Lord when they reached us! Our Lord! Pour out on us patience and constancy, and take our souls unto thee as Muslims (who bow to thy will)! (7:126)

Said Moses to his people: "Pray for help from Allah, and (wait) in patience and constancy: for the earth is Allah's, to give as a heritage to such of His servants as He pleaseth; and the end is (best) for the righteous." (7:128)

And We made the people who were deemed weak to inherit the eastern lands and the western ones which We had blessed. And the good word of thy Lord was fulfilled in the Children of Israel - because of their patience. And We destroyed what Pharaoh and his people had wrought and what they had built. (7:137)

And obey Allah and His Messenger and dispute not one with another, lest you get weak-hearted and your power depart; and be steadfast. Surely Allah is with the steadfast. (8:46)

Follow thou the inspiration sent unto thee, and be patient and constant, till Allah do decide: for He is the best to decide. (10:109)

Except those who are patient and do good. For them is forgiveness and a great reward. (11:11)

Such are some of the stories of the unseen, which We have revealed unto thee: before this, neither thou nor thy people knew them. So persevere patiently: for the End is for those who are righteous. (11:49)

And be steadfast in patience; for verily Allah will not suffer the reward of the righteous to perish. (11:115)

We sent Moses with Our signs (and the command). "Bring out thy people from the depths of darkness into light, and teach them to remember the Days of Allah." Verily in this there are Signs for such as are firmly patient and constant, grateful and appreciative. (14:5)

"No reason have we why we should not put our trust on Allah. Indeed He Has guided us to the Ways we (follow). We shall certainly bear with patience all the hurt you may cause us. For those who put their trust should put their trust on Allah." (14:12)

(They are) those who persevere in patience, and put their trust on their Lord. (16:42)

But verily thy Lord, to those who leave their homes after trials and persecutions, and who thereafter strive and fight for the faith and patiently persevere, Thy Lord, after all this is oft-forgiving, Most Merciful. (16:110)

And if you take your turn, then punish with the like of that with which you were afflicted. But if you show patience, it is certainly best for the patient. And be patient and thy patience is not but by (the help of) Allah, and grieve not for them, nor be in distress for what they plan. Surely Allah is with those who keep their duty and those who do good (to others). (16:126-127)

Lord of the heavens and the earth and what is between them, so serve Him and be patient in His service. Knowest thou any one equal to Him? (19:65)

So bear patiently what they say, and celebrate the praise of thy Lord before the rising of the sun and before its setting, and glorify (Him) during the hours of the night and parts of the day, that thou mayest be well pleased. (20:130)

And Ishmael and Idris and Dhu-l-Kifl; all were of the patient ones. (21:85)

And We did not send before thee any messengers but they surely ate food and went about in the markets. And We make some of you a trial for others. Will you bear patiently? And thy Lord is ever Seeing. (25:20)

So be patient; surely the promise of Allah is true; and let not those disquiet thee who have no certainty. (30:60)

And We appointed, from among them, leaders, giving guidance under Our command, so long as they persevered with patience and continued to have faith in Our Signs. (32:24)

Bear patiently what they say, and remember Our servant David, the possessor power. He ever turned (to Allah). (38:17)

And take in thy hand few worldly goods and earn goodness therewith and incline not to falsehood. Surely We found him patient; most excellent the servant! Surely he (ever) turned (to Us). (38:44)

So be patient; surely the promise of Allah is true; and ask protection for thy sin and celebrate the praise of thy Lord in the evening and the morning. (40:55)

So persevere in patience; for the Promise of Allah is true: and whether We show thee (in this life) some part of what We promise them, or We take thy soul (to Our Mercy) (before that), (in any case) it is to Us that they shall (all) return. (40:77)

And none is granted it but those who are patient, and none is granted it but the owner of a mighty good fortune. (41:35)

If it be His Will He can still the Wind: then would they become motionless on the back of the (ocean). Verily in this are Signs for everyone who patiently perseveres and is grateful. (42:33)

But indeed if any show patience and forgive, that would truly be an exercise of courageous will and resolution in the conduct of affairs. (42:43)

So have patience, as men of resolution, the messengers, had patience, and seek not to hasten on for them (their doom). On the day when they see that which they are promised, (it will be) as if they had not tarried save an hour of the day. (Thine is) to deliver. Shall then any be destroyed save the transgressing people? (46:35)

And We shall try you until We test those among you who strive their utmost and persevere in patience; and We shall try your reported (mettle). (47:31)

If only they had patience until thou couldst come out to them, it would be best for them: but Allah is Oft-Forgiving, Most Merciful. (49:5)

"Burn ye therein: the same is it to you whether ye bear it with patience, or not: Ye but receive the recompense of your (own) deeds." (52:16)

And wait patiently for the judgment of thy Lord, for surely thou art before Our eyes, and celebrate the praise of thy Lord, when thou risest. (52:48)

So wait with patience for the Command of thy Lord, and be not like the Companion of the Fish, when he cried out in agony. (68:48)

Therefore do thou hold Patience, a Patience of beautiful (contentment). (70:5)

And have patience with what they say, and leave them with noble (dignity). (73:10)

And for the sake of thy Lord, be patient. (74:7)

Then will he be of those who believe, and enjoin patience, (constancy, and self-restraint), and enjoin deeds of kindness and compassion. (90:17)

Except such as have Faith, and do righteous deeds, and (join together) in the mutual teaching of Truth, and of Patience and Constancy. (103:3)

For Patience

... with you must vanish: what is with Allah will endure. And We ... certainly bestow, on those who patiently persevere, their reward ... ng to the best of their actions. (16:96)

... every nation We appointed acts of devotion that they might ... the name of Allah on what He has given them of the cattle ... peds. So your God is One God, therefore to Him should you ... And give good news to the humble, Whose hearts tremble when ... is mentioned, and who are patient in their afflictions, and who keep ... er, and spend of what We have given them. (22:34-35)

... have rewarded them this day because they were patient, that they ... achievers. (23:111)

... are the ones who will be rewarded with the highest place in ... because of their patient constancy: therein shall they be met with ... ons and peace. (25:75)

... will they be given their reward, for that they have persevered, that ... ert Evil with Good, and that they spend (in charity) out of what ... e given them. (28:54)

... se who believe and work deeds of righteousness - to them shall ... e a Home in Heaven, lofty mansions beneath which flow rivers, ... therein for aye; an excellent reward for those who do (good)! ... who persevere in patience, and put their trust, in their Lord and ... her. (29:58-59)

... the men who submit and the women who submit, and the ... ng men and the believing women, and the truthful men and the ... women, and the patient men and the patient women, and the ... men and the humble women, and the charitable men and the ... le women, and the fasting men and the fasting women, and the ... ho guard their chastity and the women who guard, and the men ... member Allah much and the women who remember - Allah has ... d for them forgiveness and a mighty reward. (33:35)

Say: O My servants who believe; keep your duty to your Lord. For those who do good in this world is good, and Allah's earth is spacious. Truly the steadfast will be paid their reward without measure. (39:10)

And because they were patient and constant, He will reward them with a Garden and (garments of) silk. (76:12)

ADVERSITY & TRIALS

And when We delivered you from Pharaoh's people, who subjected you to severe torment, killing your sons and sparing your women, and in this there was a great trial from your Lord. (2:49)

And when his Lord tried Abraham with certain commands he fulfilled them. He said: Surely I will make thee a leader of men. (Abraham) said: And of my offspring? My covenant does not include the wrongdoers, said He. (2:124)

And We shall certainly try you with something of fear and hunger and loss of property and lives and fruits. And give good news to the patient. (2:155)

Or do you think that you will enter the Garden, while there has not yet befallen you the like of what befell those who have passed before you. Distress and affliction befell them and they were shaken violently, so that the Messenger and those who believed with him said: When will the help of Allah come? Now surely the help of Allah is nigh! (2:214)

So when Saul set out with the forces, he said: surely Allah will try you with a river. Whoever drinks from it, he is not of me, and whoever tastes it not, he is surely of me, except he who takes a handful with his hand. But they drank of it save a few of them. So when he had crossed it, he and those who believed with him, they said: We have today no power against Goliath and his forces. Those who were sure that they would meet their Lord said: How often has a small party vanquished a numerous host by Allah's permission! And Allah is with the steadfast. (2:249)

Do you think that you will enter the Garden while Allah has not yet known those from among you who strive hard (nor) known the steadfast? (3:142)

Then after grief He sent down security on you, slumber overcoming a party of you, while (there was) another party whom their own souls had rendered anxious - they entertained about Allah thoughts of ignorance quite unjustly. They said: Have we any hand in the affair? Say: The affair is wholly (in the hands) of Allah. They hide within their souls that which they would not reveal to thee. They say: Had we any hand in the affair, we would not have been slain here. Say: Had you remained in your houses, those for whom slaughter was ordained would have gone forth to the places where they would be slain. And (this happened) that Allah might test what was in your breasts and that He might purge what was in your hearts. And Allah is Knower of what is in the breasts. (3:154)

You will certainly be tried in your property and your persons. And you will certainly hear from those who have been given the Book before you and from the idolaters much abuse. And if you are patient and keep your duty, surely this is an affair of great resolution. (3:186)

And We have revealed to thee the Book with the truth, verifying that which is before it of the Book and a guardian over it, so judge between them by what Allah has revealed, and follow not their low desires (turning away) from the truth that has come to thee. For every one of you We appointed a law and a way. And if Allah had pleased He would have made you a single people, but that He might try you in what He gave you. So vie one with another in virtuous deeds. To Allah you will all return, so He will inform you of that wherein you differed. (5:48)

O you who believe, Allah will certainly try you in respect of some game which your hands and your lances can reach, that Allah may know who fears Him in secret. Whoever exceeds the limit after this, for him is a painful chastisement. (5:94)

And thus do We try some of them by others so that they say: Are these they upon whom Allah has conferred benefit from among us? Does not Allah best know the grateful? (6:53)

It is He Who hath made you (His) agents, inheritors of the earth: He hath raised you in ranks, some above others: that He may try you in the gifts He hath given you: for thy Lord is quick in punishment: yet He is indeed Oft-forgiving, Most Merciful. (6:165)

And when We delivered you from Pharaoh's people, who subjected you to severe torment, killing your sons and sparing your women. And therein was a great trial from your Lord. (7:141)

And Moses chose seventy of his people for Our place of meeting: when they were seized with violent quaking, he prayed: "O my Lord! If it had been Thy will Thou couldst have destroyed, long before, both them and me: wouldst Thou destroy us for the deeds of the foolish ones among us? This is no more than Thy trial: by it Thou causest whom Thou wilt to stray, and Thou leadest whom Thou wilt into the right path. Thou art our Protector: so forgive us and give us Thy mercy, for Thou art the best of those who forgive. (7:155)

And ask them about the town which stood by the sea. When they violated the Sabbath, when their fish came to them on their Sabbath day on the surface, and when it was not their Sabbath they came not to them. Thus did We try them because they transgressed. (7:163)

And ask them about the town which stood by the sea. When they violated the Sabbath, when their fish came to them on their Sabbath day on the surface, and when it was not their Sabbath they came not to them. Thus did We try them because they transgressed. (8:17)

And know ye that your possessions and your progeny are but a trial; and that it is Allah with Whom lies your highest reward. (8:28)

And know that whatever you acquire in war, a fifth of it is for Allah and for the Messenger and for the near of kin and the orphans and the needy and the wayfarer, if you believe in Allah and in that which We revealed to Our servant, on the day of Discrimination, the day on which the two parties met. And Allah is Possessor of power over all things. (8:41)

And among them is he who says: Excuse me and try me not. Surely into trial have they already fallen, and truly hell encompasses the disbelievers. (9:49)

See they not that they are tried once or twice in every year, yet they repent not, nor do they mind. (9:126)

And He it is Who created the heavens and the earth in six periods; and His Throne of Power is ever on water that He might manifest (the good qualities in) you whoever of you is best in deeds. And if thou sayest, You shall surely be raised up after death, those who disbelieve say: This is nothing but clear deceit. (11:7)

And if We make man taste mercy from Us, then withdraw it from him, he is surely despairing, ungrateful. And if We make him taste a favor after distress has afflicted him, he says: The evils are gone away from me. Certainly he is exultant, boastful, Except those who are patient and do good. For them is forgiveness and a great reward. (11:9-11)

And when Moses said to his people: Call to mind Allah's favour to you, when He delivered you from Pharaoh's people, who subjected you to severe torment, and slew your sons and spared your women. And therein was a great trial from your Lord. (14:6)

And be not like a woman who breaks into untwisted strands the yarn which she has spun, after it has become strong. Nor take your oaths to practice deception between yourselves, lest one party should be more numerous than another: for Allah will test you by this; and on the Day of Judgment He will certainly make clear to you (the truth of) that wherein ye disagree. (16:92)

But verily thy Lord, to those who leave their homes after trials and persecutions, and who thereafter strive and fight for the faith and patiently persevere, Thy Lord, after all this is oft-forgiving, Most Merciful. (16:110)

And when We said to thee: Surely thy Lord encompasses men. And We made not the vision which We showed thee but a trial for men, as also the tree cursed in the Qur'an. And We warn them, but it only adds to their great inordinacy. (17:60)

That which is on earth we have made but as a glittering show for the earth, in order that We may test them as to which of them are best in conduct. (18:7)

...oul shall have a taste of death: and We test you by evil and by
...by way of trial. To Us must ye return. (21:35)

...re among men some who serve Allah, as it were, on the verge: if
...befalls them, they are, therewith, well content; but if a trial comes
...them, they turn on their faces: they lose both this world and the
...other: that is loss for all to see! (22:11)

...not the calling among you of the Messenger as your calling one of
...Allah indeed knows those who steal away from among you,
...ing themselves. So let those who go against his order beware, lest
...afflict them or there befall them a painful chastisement. (24:63)

...he messengers whom We sent before thee were all (men) who ate
...and walked through the streets: We have made some of you as a
...others: will ye have patience? For Allah is One Who sees (all
...(25:20)

...id: We augur evil of thee and those with thee. He said: Your evil
...is with Allah; nay, you are a people who are tried. (27:47)

...were the believers tried and they were shaken with a severe
...(33:11)

...n harm afflicts a man he calls upon Us; then, when We give him
...from Us, he says: I have been given it only by means of
...ledge. Nay, it is a trial, but most of them know not. (39:49)

...rtainly We tried before them Pharaoh's people and a nobel
...ger came to them. (44:17)

...rtainly We shall try you, till We know those among you who strive
...nd the steadfast, and manifest your news. (47:31)

...ly We sent Our messengers with clear arguments, and sent down
...m the Book and the measure, that men may conduct themselves
...quity. And We sent down iron, wherein is great violence and

advantages to men, and that Allah may know who helps Him and His messengers, unseen. Surely Allah is Strong, Mighty. (57:25)

Our Lord, make us not a trial for those who disbelieve, and forgive us, our Lord. Surely Thou art the Mighty, the Wise. (60:5)

Your wealth and your children are only a trial, and Allah -- with Him is a great reward. (64:15)

He Who created Death and Life, that He may try which of you is best in deed: and He is the Exalted in Might, Oft-Forgiving. (67:2)

So that We may try them thereby. And whoever turns away from the reminder of his Lord, He will make him enter into an afflicting chastisement. (72:17)

Verily We created Man from a drop of mingled sperm, in order to try him: So We gave him (the gifts), of Hearing and Sight. (76:2)

Now, as for man, when his Lord trieth him, giving him honour and gifts, then saith he, (puffed up), "My Lord hath honoured me." But when He trieth him, restricting his subsistence for him, then saith he (in despair), "My Lord hath humiliated me!" (89:15-16)

HADITH
SAYINGS OF PROPHET MUHAMMAD (SAW)

This Section of Hadith Literature, Prayers of the Prophets and Spiritual Care Commentary is excerpted from the excellent book *The Necessity and Benefits of Trials and Tribulations* by Kalamazad Mohammad.

Prayers of the Prophets

1. Prayer of Prophet Adam and his wife, Eve, after having approached the forbidden tree: They said: Our Lord, we have wronged ourselves; and if Thou forgive us not, and have (not) mercy on us, we shall certainly be of the losers (7:23).

2. Prayer of Prophet Jonah when he left his people in wrath and fell into distress: And Dhu-I-Nun, when he went away in wrath, and he thought that We would not straiten him, so he called out among afflictions: There is no god but Thou, Glory be to Thee! Surely I am of the sufferers of Loss (21:87).

3. Prayer of Prophet Job when afflicted in both family and property: And Job, when he cried to his Lord: Distress has afflicted me! And Thou art the most Merciful of those who show mercy (21:83).

4. Prayer of Prophet Zacharias for a righteous son: A mention of the mercy of thy Lord, crying in secret. He said: My Lord, my bones are weakened, and my head flares with hoariness, and I have never been unsuccessful in my prayer to Thee, my Lord, and I fear my kinsfolk after me, and my wife is barren, so grant me from Thyself an heir who should inherit me and inherit of the Children of Jacob, and make him my Lord, acceptable (to Thee) (19:2-6).

5. Prayer of Prophet Moses after fleeing from Pharaoh and reaching Midian: So, he watered (their sheep) for them, then went back to

the shade, and said: My Lord, I stand in need of whatever good Thou mayest sent to me (28:24).

6. Prayer of the holy Prophet Muhammad (peace and blessings of Allah be upon him) after he was rejected at Taif, abused and stoned: "O Lord, I make my complaint unto Thee of my helplessness and frailty and of my insignificance before mankind. But Thou the Lord of the poor and feeble and Thou art my Lord. Into whose hand wilt Thou abandon me? Into the hands of strangers that beset me round about? Or of the enemy Thou hast given at home to have the mastery over me? I seek refuge in the light of Thy countenance."

From the Hadith

As regard afflictions, the Hadith consoles us:

1. Lady Ayesha reported: "I did not see anybody on whom pain was more severe than on the Messenger of Allah."

2. "To whomsoever Allah intends good, he gets some afflictions from Him."

3. "There is no Muslim on whom a calamity of illness falls or what is besides it, except that Allah drops his sins just as a tree drops its leaves."

4. "No Muslim is afflicted by difficulty, continuous pain, anxiety, grief, injury, or care, or even by a thorn with which he is pierced, without Allah thereby making an atonement for his sins."

5. The magnitude of reward goes along with the magnitude of the trial, and when the Almighty and Glorious loves a people, He puts them to trials. So whoever is pleased, there is pleasure for him, and whoever is displeased, there is displeasure for him.

6. "When a Muslim is tried with a disease in his body, it is said to the angel: 'Write for him the good actions he used to do.' If he

cures him, He washes him and purifies him (of all sins); and if He takes his life, He forgives him and shows mercy to him."

7. "When Allah has previously decreed for a servant a rank which he has not attained by his actions, He afflicts him in his body, or in his wealth,, or in his children, and he keeps patience over that, till He takes him to the abode which went in advance for him from Allah.

8. "The Messenger of Allah was asked: 'Who among men is the foremost in trouble?' 'Prophets,' he replied, 'then their followers and then their followers.'"

9. "A man is tried in proportion to his religion. If he has firmness in religion, his disaster becomes severe, and if he has weakness in his religion, it becomes easy for him. He continues in that way till he walks upon the earth without sin."

(The above hadith were taken from Maulana Fazlul Karim's translation of Mishkat al-Masabih, Book 1 section 7 chapter 111.)

10. "If anyone comforts one who has been afflicted he will have a reward equivalent to his."

11. "No pair of Muslims will lose three of their children by death without Allah bringing them into Paradise by His great mercy." He was asked if that applied if they lost two, and he said it did. He was also asked if it applied if they lost one, and he said it did.

12. "The believing man or woman continues to have affliction in person, property and children so that they may finally meet God free from sin." (Timidhi)

13. The Holy Prophet said that Allah said: "When I afflict a servant of Mine who is a believer and he praises me for the affliction I have brought upon him, he will rise from that couch of his as sinless as he was the day he mother gave him birth. I fettered and

afflicted my servant, so record for him what you were recording for him when he was well." (Ahmad)

14. "It is remarkable that everything turns out well for a believer while that applies only to a believer. If happiness befalls him he gives thanks and it turns out well for him, and if misfortune befalls him he shows endurance and it turns out well for him." (Muslim)

15. "The strong believer is better and dearer to God than the weak believer. In all that is good be eager for what benefits you, seek help in God, and do not be too weak to do so. If any affliction comes to you do not say: 'If I had done such and such, such and such would have happened," but say: "God decrees and what He wishes He does, for 'if I had' provides an opening for the deeds of the devil." (Muslim)

16. "Part of the happiness of a son of Adam consists in his pleasure with what God has decreed for him, part of the misery of a son of Adam consists in his abandonment of asking God's blessing, and part of the misery of a son of Adam consists in his displeasure with what God has decreed for him." (Muslim)

(The above hadith were taken from Robson's translation of Mishkat al-Masabih.)

Lessons from the Qur'an

Let us now turn our attention to Mr. N.A. Faruqui's dars-ul-Qur'an (lessons from the Qur'an) on 2:153-157 of the Holy Qur'an.

O you, who believe, seek assistance through patience and prayer; surely Allah is with the patient. And speak not of those who are slain in Allah's way as dead. Nay, (they are) alive, but you perceive not. And we shall certainly try you with something of fear and hunger and loss of property and lives and fruits. And give good news to the patient, who, when a misfortune befalls them say: Surely we are Allah's and to Him we shall return. Those are they on who are blessings and mercy form their Lord, and those are the followers of the right course.

...verses deal with the subject of suffering and the importance of ...perseverance in it, and for this reason I thought it important to ...them in my lesson. The Holy Qur'an sheds light on the topic of ...d afflictions and tells us that they befall us in three ways.

...when any prophet comes, or now that prophethood has come to ...when mujaddids or other commissioned ones make their ...nce, then severe opposition is raised against them and their ...s, and attempts are even made o their lives. In short, affliction ...fliction of various kinds befall those who accept the truth.

...difficulties result from man's evil deeds, errors or heedlessness, ...Holy Qur'an explains later:

And whatever misfortune befalls you, it is on account of
what our hand have wrought and He pardons much.
(42:30)

...r that the remedy for this kind of affliction, besides *sabr* ...erance), is *taubah* (repentance), *istighfar* (seeking forgiveness ...tection from sin), and self-reformation.

...mes it is very difficult to make a distinction between these three ...f affliction. For this reason, piety and caution demand that ...er the kind of difficulty that may attend, besides *sabr*, one should ...*taubah* and *istighfar* and self-reformation. If the trial does arise ...of one's own doing, then its coming can serve a higher purpose; ...one's improvement and one's moral and spiritual perfection, just ...is purified when it passes through the crucible of fire. This is one ...fects of misfortune.

...ligious person considers difficulties as accidental happenings or ...events and so displays impatience and restlessness when smitten. ...rts to alcohol or some other king of intoxicant as he vainly tries ...t the misfortune. Sometimes, some people even commit suicide. ...Qur'an, full of wisdom, tells us:

No calamity befalls except through the command or the
permission of Allah. (64:11)

For this reason, one must endure troubles with courage, *sabr*, *taubah* and
istighfar, and one must solicitously look after correcting one's self, just
in case (may Allah forbid) those burdens have come about as a
punishment for one's evil deeds.

To call for help when affliction strikes is inherent in man's nature, and
as every difficulty comes through Allah's command or His permission,
it is entirely in accord with his nature to call upon Him for help. Let us
now examine in what manner one should ask for that assistance.

The first category of difficulty which I mentioned above is that which
befalls the sent ones of God or the acceptors of truth. So, as those who
accept truth are unfortunately always small in number and weak in
means, while their opponents exceed them greatly in numbers and power
and they are ever on the boil to hurt and even destroy the righteous ones,
the necessity, nay, the restless thirst of seeking assistance, is created in
the hearts of the acceptors of truth. And who is their helper except Allah?
Therefore He instructs us (in the first verse of this lesson) to seek
assistance but with patience, that is, to be patient in trials and afflictions
would in itself bring the help of Allah, Most High.

Nonetheless, it is in the nature of man to call for help. That is why Allah.
Most High, commands us to call on Him through *du'a* (supplication) and
salah (prayer). If the believers in Truth are urged to bear patience, it is
because by accepting Truth, whatever trials come, they come so that
man's lip profession of faith may be driven into his heart like a nail.
Furthermore, faith penetrates the very veins and fibres of man provided
that he endures afflictions with fortitude and remains firm in his
convictions. And if it to such a person Allah gave permission to call on
Him through *du'a* and *salah*, it is because *du'a* an *salah* establish and
reinforce the bond between man and Allah, and as the affliction
lengthens, he increases in strength and that is the greatest benefit a
believer can derive from difficulties. For this reason, truth indeed comes
so that the slaves of Allah may meet Him. Furthermore, bowing before
Allah brings comfort to the heart of a believer and ultimately feelings of

delight and ecstasy come, and that is the highest bounty in this life and the next. Those who believe and whose hearts find rest in the remembrance of Allah. Now surely in Allah's remembrance do hearts find rest. (13:28)

So, if in spite of man's fortitude and sincere appeals to Allah the difficulties do not give away, do not think that Allah is not a man's side or that his supplications have been in vain. For this reason, the works: Certainly Allah is with the patient are repeated. So make *du'a* and preserves patiently, because patience is an outstanding attribute of Allah and both the Holy Qur'an and the Hadith command us to acquire the qualities of Allah, Most High.

What a great honor it is for man to be given the opportunity to colour himself with colours of Allah, and who can be more patient than Allah? We take Allah's colour, and who is better than Allah coloring. (2:138). Today, right in front of His eyes there are so many peoples of the world who deny His existence; not only the peoples in communist countries, but in Europe and Americas well, the cry has been raised and this has spread to all parts of the globe, that God (may Allah forbid!) never existed, and even if He did, then He is now dead. Those who do not display this rudeness and impertinence attribute Partners to Allah, Most High, and worship an idol which they have made with their own hands, or they worship an animal, the cow or they take as God creation of His – a dead human being (Prophet Jesus). That, too, is tantamount to rudeness and insolence. In addition, the most heinous sins, evils and mischief are committed right in front of God's eyes and see how He bears all this with patience and determination. If He were not so merciful and forbearing, then the whole. Many of the accepters of truth have been murdered. Were their lives in vain or their efforts wasted? Certainly not! We are told not to refer to them as dead for they have, in fact, attained that exalted and everlasting life which it is impossible to surpass. They have been delivered from this life and its sorrows, illnesses, hunger and pain and have gone straight into the everlasting garden of bliss. In fact, they are to be envied!

The second class of afflictions are those that are from Allah as a decree or as a trial, by means of different kinds of fear, hunger, poverty or the loss of wealth and lives or the fruits of labor. These difficulties have been decreed as a form of trial. The purpose of a trial, when Allah is the One Who sends it, is to manifest the hidden condition of man; that is, his inner virtues or weakness. And be not weak-hearted, nor grieve. (3:139). For example, if difficulty befalls a man and in order to extricate himself he tells a lie or accepts a bribe or breaks his promise, etc., then in this way his concealed weaknesses are brought into the open so that he may reform himself before death comes and carries him off leaving for him no remedy but Hell. On the other, if a person bears with stoicism those God-ordained trials, there develop in his character such high morals that were non-existent before. This is a manifestation of hidden beauties. Just as a tree that possesses within if flowers and fruits reside in man's personality are the very ones which will assume the form of lovely flowers and fruits of his garden in the next life.

This is why Allah commands and give news to those who bear the slings and arrows of faith with steadfastness. What good news is, will be disclosed later. But before that, who are the patient ones who, when god-given trials befall, say: "We are the property of Allah. He can do whatever He likes with us"? And if we have lost something or some damage is done then that is only a trifle, for we, ourselves, have to rerun to Him and if he is pleased with us, He will compensate us over and above in that everlasting home which He will bestow on us. In any case, everything in this life has to be lost when death comes to us. But over and above this, in this very life He says that such people will be granted *maghfirah* (forgiveness) and *rahmah* (mercy).

Maghfirah is Allah's protection. Protection from what? From the evil consequences of man's sins, from weaknesses or heedlessness or from punishment for past sins or from committing those same sins in the future because of human weaknesses. Whenever man commits a sin or exhibits some weakness or carelessness, then the danger of falling into it again is possible. For example, if a person steals once, it becomes easy for him to do it a second time. So, the patient man does not only receive Allah's protection, but Allah says that His spiritual graces descend on him. Spiritual graces are the real blessings, for worldly bounties come to an end during man's lifetime or certainly when he dies. But spiritual favours accompany his soul into the next life - the everlasting one - and there they will assume the form of manifest blessings.

Also mentioned is another great blessing for the patient, and that is contained in Surah Al-Fatihah.

Guide us to the right path.

The guidance is really finding Allah, Himself. Finding Allah is indeed the purpose of man's existence or creation and there is no bigger boon that man can get than that of meeting the Most High. Then He says that these favoured ones will be guided along the straight path that will lead them in this very life to Allah, Himself, like the prophets, the truthful and the saints who meet Allah here on earth. But these are the ones who suffer the most afflictions. For this reason, my friends, do not be anxious in times of distress, but bear them with fortitude in order that you may meet Allah, Most High.

Wherever you are, death will overtake you, though you are in towers, raised high. And if good befalls them, they say: This is from Allah; and if a misfortune befalls them, they say: This is from thee. Say: All is from Allah. But what is the matter with these people that they make no effort to understand anything? Whatever good befalls thee (O man), it is from Allah, and whatever misfortune befalls thee, it is from thyself. And We have sent thee (O Prophet) to mankind as a Messenger. And Allah is sufficient as a witness. (4:78-79)

THE BIBLE AND COMPARATIVE RELIGIONS

Help and Deliverance

One who has a true hold on life, when he walks on land does not meet tigers or wild buffaloes; in battle he is not touched by weapons of war. Indeed, a buffalo that attacked him would find nothing for his horns to butt, a tiger would find nothing for its claws to tear, a weapon would find no place for its blade to lodge. And why? Because such men have no "death-spot" in them.
- Taoism. Tao Te Ching 50

He who dwells in the shelter of the Most High, who abides in the shadow of the Almighty, will say to the Lord, "My refuge and my fortress; my God, in whom I trust." For he will deliver you from the snare of the fowler, and from the deadly pestilence; he will cover you with his pinions, and under his wings you will find refuge; his faithfulness is a shield and buckler. You will not fear the terror of the night, nor the arrow that flies by day, nor the pestilence that stalks in darkness, nor the destruction that wastes at noonday. A thousand may fall at your side, ten thousand at your right hand; but it will not come near you. You will only look with your eyes and see the recompense of the wicked. Because you have made the Lord your refuge, the Most High your habitation, no evil shall befall you, no scourge come near your tent. For he will give his angels charge of you to guard you in all your ways. On their hands they will bear you up, lest you dash your foot against a stone. You will tread on the lion and the adder, the young lion and the serpent you will trample under foot.
- Judaism and Christianity.   Bible, Psalm 91:1-13

If God gives you a cup of wine and an evil-minded person kicks it over, He fills it up for you again.
- African Traditional Religions. Akan Proverb (Ghana)

A king is not saved by his great army, a warrior is not delivered by his great strength. The war horse is a vain hope for victory, and by its great might it cannot save. Behold, the eye of the Lord is on those who fear him, on those who hope in his steadfast love, that he may deliver their

...m death, and keep them alive in famine. Our soul waits for the
...e is our help and our shield.
...m and Christianity. Bible, Psalm 33:16-20

...our refuge and strength, a very present help in trouble. Therefore
...not fear though the earth should change, though the mountains
...the heart of the sea; though its waters roar and foam, though the
...ins tremble with its tumult. - Judaism and Christianity. Bible,
...6:1-3

...your fight to Olodumare and look on, for he is defender of the
...less.
...Traditional Religions. Yoruba Proverb (Nigeria)

...ou not known? Have you not heard? The Lord is the everlasting
...Creator of the ends of the earth. He does not grow weary, he
...tire, his understanding is unsearchable. He gives strength to the
...and to him who has no might he increases strength. Youths may
...d be weary, and young men may fall, exhausted; but they who
...the Lord shall renew their strength. They shall mount up with
...ike eagles, they shall run and not be weary. They shall walk and
...w faint.
...m and Christianity. Bible, Isaiah 40:28-31

...the lord bestow His might on the tiny ant, Hordes million-strong
...destroy. Whomsoever He Himself sends not to death, He guards
...strength of His arm. Despite all his efforts, All man's endeavors
...itless. None other is savior or destroyer: He Himself is guardian
...beings.   Thou man! Why all this anxiety?   Says Nanak,
...iplate Him who is beyond thy understanding, Who is so
...ful.
...m. Adi Granth, Gauri Sukhmani

...little ability, too, by depending upon the great, may prosper; A
...water is a little thing, but when will it dry away if united to a

...hism. Elegant Sayings 173

To those who have conformed themselves to the Way, the Way readily lends its power. To those who have conformed themselves to the power, the power readily lends more power.
- Taoism. Tao Te Ching

God, the Lord, is my strength; he makes my feet like hind's feet, he makes me tread upon high places.
- Judaism and Christianity. Bible, Habakkuk 3:19

If God is for us, who can be against us?
- Christianity. Bible, Romans 8:31

United with me, you shall overcome all difficulties by my grace.
- Hinduism. Bhagavad Gita 18:58

Not by might, nor by power, but by my Spirit, says the Lord of hosts.
- Judaism and Christianity. Bible, Zechariah 4:6

Suffering As The Refiner's Fire

Welcome to Thy wrath and to Thy glow! Our welcome be to Thy flame! Let Thy missiles burn our enemies, be our purifier, be gracious to us!
- Hinduism. Yajur Veda 36:20

Just as a great conflagration can burn up all things, so does Buddha's field of blessings burn up all fabrication.
- Buddhism. Garland Sutra 10

I will put this third into the fire, and refine them as one refines silver, and test them as gold is tested.
- Judaism and Christianity. Bible, Zechariah 13:9

We rejoice in our sufferings, knowing that suffering produces endurance, and endurance produces character, and character produces hope, and hope does not disappoint us, because God's love has been poured into our hearts.
- Christianity. Bible, Romans 5:3-5

Yet the suffering involved in my awakening will have a limit; It is like the suffering of having an incision made in order to remove and destroy greater pain. Even doctors eliminate illness with unpleasant medical treatments, so in order to overcome manifold sufferings I should be able to put up with some discomfort. But the Supreme Physician does not employ common medical treatments such as these, With an extremely gentle technique He remedies all the greatest sins.
- Guide to the Bodhisattva's Way of Life

Mencius said, "Shun rose from the fields; Fu Yeh was raised to office from among the builders; Chiao Ke from amid the fish and salt; Kuan Chung from the hands of the prison officer; Sun Shu-ao from the sea and Po-li His from the market. That is why Heaven, when it is about to place a great burden on a man, always first tests his resolution, exhausts his frame and makes him suffer starvation and hardship, frustrates his efforts so as to shake him from his mental lassitude, toughen his nature, and make good his deficiencies."
- Confucianism. Mencius VI.B.15

And to keep me from being too elated by the abundance of revelations, a thorn was given me in the flesh, a messenger of Satan, to harass me, to keep me from being too elated. Three times I [Paul] besought the Lord about this, that it should leave me; but he said to me, "My grace is sufficient for you, for my power is made perfect in weakness." I will all the more gladly boast of my weaknesses, that the power of Christ may rest upon me. For the sake of Christ, then, I am content with weaknesses, insults, hardships, persecutions, and calamities; for when I am weak, then I am strong.
- Christianity. Bible, 2 Corinthians 12:7-10

My brethren, take the prophets, who spoke in the name of the Lord, as an example of suffering and patience. Indeed we count them blessed who endure. You have heard of the perseverance of Job and seen the end *intended by* the Lord - that the Lord is very compassionate and merciful.
- Christianity. Bible, James 5:10-11

For this *is* commendable, if because of conscience toward God one endures grief, suffering wrongfully. For what credit *is it* if, when you

are beaten for your faults, you take it patiently? But when you do good and suffer, if you take it patiently, this *is* commendable before God. For to this you were called, because Christ also suffered for us, leaving us an example, that you should follow His steps: *"Who committed no sin, nor was deceit found in His mouth";* who, when He was reviled, did not revile in return; when He suffered, He did not threaten, but committed *Himself* to Him who judges righteously;
- Christianity. Bible, 1 Peter 2:19-23

And you have forgotten the exhortation which speaks to you as to sons: *"My son, do not despise the chastening of the Lord, Nor be discouraged when you are rebuked by Him; For whom the Lord loves He chastens, And scourges every son whom He receives."*
- Christianity. Bible, Hebrews 12:5-6

You should know in your heart that as a man chastens his son, *so* the Lord your God chastens you.   Therefore you shall keep the commandments of the Lord your God, to walk in His ways and to fear Him. For the Lord your God is bringing you into a good land, a land of brooks of water, of fountains and springs, that flow out of valleys and hills; a land of wheat and barley, of vines and fig trees and pomegranates, a land of olive oil and honey; a land in which you will eat bread without scarcity, in which you will lack nothing; a land whose stones *are* iron and out of whose hills you can dig copper.
- Christianity. Bible, Deuteronomy 8:5-9

HOLY QUR'AN TRANSLATOR
A. YUSUF ALI NOTES ON THE PSALMS

David's distinction was the Psalms, which are still extant. Though their present form may possibly be different from the original and they do undoubtedly include Psalms not written by David, the collection contains much devotional poetry of a high order. (21:105)

Sorrow and suffering may (if we take them rightly) turn out to be the best gifts of Allah to us. According to the Psalms (94:12) "Blessed is the man whom Thou chastenest, O Lord!" Through suffering we learn humility, the antidote to many vices and the fountain of many virtues. But if we take them the wrong way, we grumble and complain, we become fainthearted; and Satan gets his opportunity to exploit us by putting forward the alluring pleasures of his Vanity Fair.

The spiritual gifts with which the prophets came may themselves take different forms, according to the needs of the world and the times in which they lived, as judged by the wisdom of Allah. A striking example here given is the gift of song and music as given to David, but it implies no superiority of David over others. David was given the Zabur, the psalter or Psalms, intended to be sung for the worship of Allah and the celebration of Allah's praise.

Whatever is in the heavens and the earth celebrates the praises of Allah: 17:44; 57:1; 16:48-50, and 22:18. Even the "thunder repeateth His praises." 13:13. All nature ever sings the praises of Allah. David sang in his Psalms, 148:7-10: "Praise the Lord from the earth, ye . . . mountains and all hills . . . creeping things and flying fowl!" All nature sings to Allah's glory, in unison with David, and angels, and men of God. (See Surah 34:10 and 38:18-19.)

23ᴿᴰ PSALMS

A Psalm of David.

The LORD *is* my shepherd;

I shall not want. He maketh me to lie down in green pastures:

He leadeth me beside the still waters. He restoreth my soul:

He leadeth me in the paths of righteousness for his name's sake.

Yea, though I walk through the valley of the shadow of death,

I will fear no evil: for thou *art* with me; thy rod and thy staff they comfort me.

Thou preparest a table before me in the presence of mine enemies:

Thou anointest my head with oil; my cup runneth over.

Surely goodness and mercy shall follow me all the days of my life:

And I will dwell in the house of the LORD forever.

- Psalms 23:1-6

THE PSALTER ITS LARGER AND DISCRETIONARY USE DESIRABLE

Excerpted from The Muhammadan Controversy
by Sir William Muir

The Psalms have been the refuge of the soul, the voice of the
rich, the song of the saint, in all generations. They are still the same,
and in privacy of the still chamber as in public ministrations of the
congregation. From the treasury of the Psalter, be his outward state
and frame what they may, the child of God is ever borrowing words
to give shape and substance to flitting thought, life to the soul, and
to heavenward aspiration.

Here is stored up Divine food, rich and abundant, for every time
and place. Something for the morning dawn, something for the busy day,
something for the dark watches of the night; something for the sick
solitary closet, something also for the thronging crowd. The
backsliding, the penitent, the weak and afflicted, the doubting and the
proud; the soul dwelling in darkness, desolate, disowned by man, or
longing to be forsaken by the Almighty; and not less, the Saint on fire
of godly zeal, hungering and thirsting after the living God, borne
upwards on wings of love and joy, each may find in the Psalms words
made, as it were, to suit his very case. And as in personal, domestic,
social life, so also in a nation's history, whether in peace or warfare,
whether the year be crowned with goodness or the staff of bread be
broken, in the day of wealth and prosperity, as well as in the night of
misery and pestilence; in short, at every turn of public life the people's
cry of sorrow or of joy will ascend, as it can no otherwise ascend, in
the Psalmist's very words. And, what is much to be observed, while
these abound with cries of anguish as well as with the "tenderest
appeals to God's compassionate love that ever trembled on human lips,"
there is yet nothing weak or morbid, nothing extravagant or strained (as
we too often see in our modern hymnody) throughout the Psalter: all is
sound and real, manly, simple, noble, and well-nerved.

SAYINGS AND QUOTATIONS

SUFFERING

"It is out of suffering that the creative power is unleashed. If you don't suffer, you can't create. So don't run from your pain, run to it. Don't run from your trial and don't turn your back on your struggle. Allah (God) says in the Qur'an that He created man to face difficulty. If you turn your back like a coward because you don't want to face the trials and tribulation that life comes up with - you'd rather drink yourself under or smoke yourself under, you'd rather commit suicide rather than to face difficulty - then you disbelieve in the Power of Allah (God) to change any reality, no matter how harsh that reality may be."
- Honorable Minister Louis Farrakhan
Good Samaritan Ecumenical Church in Tchula, MS
November 3, 2002

"God has foreordained the works to which He has called you (see Ephesians 2:10). He has been ahead of you preparing the place to which you are coming and manipulating all the resources of the universe in order that the work you do may be a part of His whole great and gracious work."
- G. Campbell Morgan

"But pain insists upon being attended to. God whispers to us in our pleasures, speaks in our conscience, but shouts in our pains: it is His megaphone to rouse a deaf world."
- C.S. Lewis

"A newborn child has to cry, for only in this way will his lungs expand. A doctor once told me of a child who could not breathe when it was born. In order to make it breathe the doctor gave it a slight blow. The mother must have thought the doctor cruel. But he was really doing the kindest thing possible. As with newborn children the lungs are contracted, so are our spiritual lungs. But through suffering God strikes us in love. Then our lungs expand and we can breathe and pray."
- Sadhu Sundar Singh

"If you suffer, thank God! - It is a sure sign that you are alive."
- Elbert Hubbard

"I say that trials and tests locate a person. In other words they determine where you are spiritually. They reveal the true condition of your heart. How you react under pressure is how the real you reacts."
 - *John Bevere*

"Life is 10% what happens to you, and 90% how you respond to it"
- *Unknown*

"The two big advantages I had at birth were to have been born wise and to have been born in poverty. "
 - *Stevie Wonder*

"Blessings alone do not open our eyes. Indeed, blessings by themselves tend to close our eyes. We do not come to know Him in the blessing, but in the breaking."
 - *Chip Brogden*

"Most people are far more prone to let the bad experiences shape their views than the good ones."
- *Rick Joyner*

"Must you continue to be your own cross? No matter which way God leads you, you change everything into bitterness by constantly brooding over everything. For the love of God, replace all this self-scrutiny with a pure and simple glance at God's goodness."
- *Saint Jeanne Chantal*

"Our problems are opportunities to discover God's solutions."
- *Unknown*

"Far too often, however, we resent and resist any interference on God's part that might deprive us of our deepest desires. Many Christians who sing, 'It is well with my soul,' are lying. It is not well with their souls because they are not persevering, and they have no intention of doing so, because they are bitter and hostile toward God and mourn over their 'victimization' at His hands. Others are little better, for they 'persevere'

NURSE FROM YOUR HOLY QUR'AN

with a cold, stony, stoic demeanor that constantly reminds God how much they are doing for Him despite His lack of reciprocity."
- *Jim Owe*

"Depression is rage spread thin."
- *Paul Tillich*

"The world is full of suffering, it is also full of overcoming it."
- *Helen Keller*

"These things I have spoken unto you, that in me ye might have peace. In the world ye shall have tribulation: but be of good cheer; I have overcome the world."
- *Jesus (John 16:33)*

"If thou art willing to suffer no adversity, how wilt thou be the friend of Christ?"
- *Thomas à Kempis*

"God will not look you over for medals, degrees, or diplomas, but for scars."
- *Elbert Hubbard*

"Better to be occasionally cheated than perpetually suspicious."
- *Unknown*

"Do not, I beseech you be troubled by the increase of forces already in dissolution. You have mistaken the hour of the night: it is already morning."
- *G.K. Chesterson*

"Grief knits two hearts in closer bonds than happiness ever can; and common sufferings are far stronger links than common joys."
- *Alphonse de Lamartine*

"It is highly significant, and indeed almost a rule, that moral courage has its source in identification through one's own sensitivity with the suffering of one's fellow human beings."

- Rollo May

"Character cannot be developed in ease and quiet. Only through experience of trial and suffering can the soul be strengthened, ambition inspired, and success achieved."
- Helen Keller

"Deep unspeakable suffering may well be called a baptism, a regeneration, the initiation into a new state."
- George Eliot

"It is through much tribulation that we enter the kingdom of Heaven."
- Acts 14:22

"Difficult times have helped me to understand better than before, how infinitely rich and beautiful life is in every way, and that so many things that one goes worrying about are of no importance whatsoever."
- Isak Dinesen

"The will of God is never exactly what you expect it to be. It may seem to be much worse, but in the end it's going to be a lot better and a lot bigger."
 - Elisabeth Elliot

"Pain is never permanent."
 - Teresa of Avila

"Most people are quite happy to suffer in silence, if they are sure everybody knows they are doing it."
- Anonymous

"Suffering, once accepted, loses its edge, for the terror of it lessens, and what remains is generally far more manageable than we had imagined."
- Leslie Hazelton

"You desire to know the art of living, my friend? It is contained in one phrase: make use of suffering."

Fredric Amiel

...ost authentic thing about us is our capacity to create, to
...me, to endure, to transform, to love and to be greater than our
...ng."
...*kri*

...ust submit to supreme suffering in order to discover the
...tion of joy."
...*Calvin*

...ring is but another name for the teaching of experience, which is
...nt of instruction and the schoolmaster of life."
...*e*

...o suffers much will know much."
...*Proverb*

...is to suffer, to survive is to find some meaning in the
...ng."
...*ta Flack*

...ffering and enduring there is no remedy, but striving and doing."
...*as Carlyle*

...have a hard time letting go of their suffering. Out of a fear of
...nown, they prefer suffering that is familiar."
...*Nhat Hanh*

...ring is everywhere. Don't ever think it isn't. So are miracles.
...ver think they aren't."
...

...ne you suffer a setback or disappointment, put your head down
...w ahead."
...*rown.*

"The sufferings that fate inflicts on us should be borne with patience, what enemies inflict with manly courage."
- *Thucydides*

"What was hard to suffer is sweet to remember."
- *Lucius Annaeus Seneca*

"If you learn from your suffering, and really come to understand the lesson you were taught, you might be able to help someone else who's now in the phase you may have just completed. Maybe that's what it's all about after all."
- *Anonymous*

"Oh, fear not in a world like this, and thou shalt know erelong, know how sublime a thing it is to suffer and be strong."
- *Henry Wadsworth Longfellow*

"Who feareth to suffer suffereth already, because he feareth."
-*Michel Eyquem de Montaigne*

"One must really have suffered oneself, to help others."
- *Mother Teresa*

"Man cannot remake himself without suffering, for he is both the marble and the sculptor."
- *Alexis Carrel*

"Wisdom comes alone through suffering."
- *Aeschylus*

"Suffering becomes beautiful when anyone bears great calamities with cheerfulness, not through insensibility but through greatness of mind."
- *Aristotle*

"Suffering is the price of being alive, and it is music and singing and art that has helped me live through some of the most difficult things that have happened to me."
- *Judy Collins*

"Man suffers most from the suffering he fears, but never appears, therefore he suffers more than god meant him to suffer."
- *Dutch Proverb*

"Suffering produces endurance, and endurance produces character, and character produces hope."
- *Romans 5:3-4*

"The most authentic thing about us is our capacity to create, to overcome, to endure, to transform, to love and to be greater than our suffering."
- *Ben Okri*

"Seeing much, suffering much, and studying much are the three pillars of learning."
- *Benjamin Disraeli*

"Sacrifice still exists everywhere, and everywhere the elect of each generation suffers for the salvation of the rest."
- *Henri Frederic Amiel*

"The person who risks nothing, does nothing, has nothing, is nothing, and becomes nothing. He may avoid suffering and sorrow, but he simply cannot learn and feel and change and grow and love and live."
- *Leo F. Buscaglia*

"If you take no risks, you will suffer no defeats. But if you take no risks, you win no victories."
- *U.S. President Richard M. Nixon*

PROBLEMS

"The desire to attain a goal brings us face to face with difficulty. When we undergo the trial of difficulty, the trial may be so intense that it extinguishes the light of the desire to attain the goal. The exertion of energy in facing and overcoming difficulty strengthens character. Each time we face Difficulty and use our faith in our Lord to overcome it, there is a reward. This reward gives us the incentive to try and try again."
- *Honorable Minister Louis Farrakhan*
Self-Improvement is the Basis for Community Development
Study Guide 3, Overcoming Difficulty

"None of us can be free of conflict and woe. Even the greatest men have had to accept disappointments as their daily bread."
- *Bernard M. Baruch*

"There is no man at any rank who is always at liberty to act as he would incline. In some quarter or other he is limited by circumstances."
- *Bonnie Blair*

"When life's problems seem overwhelming, look around and see what other people are coping with. You may consider yourself fortunate."
- *Ann Landers*

"A problem well stated is a problem half solved."
- *Charles F. Kettering*

"If we can really understand the problem, the answer will come out of it because the answer is not separate from the problem."
- *Kiddu Krishnamurti*

"The man who most vividly realizes a difficulty is the man most likely to overcome it."
- *Joseph Farrell*

"A good problem statement often includes: (a) what is known, (b) what is unknown, and (c) what is sought."

- Edward Hodnett

"You often get a better hold upon a problem by going away from it for a time and dismissing it from your mind altogether."
- Dr. Frank Crane

"When I feel difficulty coming on, I switch to another book I'm writing. When I get back to the problem, my unconscious has solved it."
 - Isaac Asimov

"You can surmount the obstacles in your path if you are determined, courageous and hard-working. Never be fainthearted. Be resolute, but never bitter . . . Permit no one to dissuade you from pursuing the goals you set for yourselves. Do not fear to pioneer, to venture down new paths of endeavor."
- Ralph J. Bunche

"Any concern too small to be turned into a prayer too small to be made into a burden."
 - Carrie Ten Boom

"When you approach a problem, strip yourself of preconceived opinions and prejudice, assemble and learn the facts of the situation, make the decision which seems to you to be the most honest, and then stick to it."
 - Chester Bowles

"No matter how big and tough a problem may be, get rid of confusion by taking one little step towards solution. Do something. Then try again. At the worst, so long as you don't do it the same way twice, you will eventually use up all the wrong ways of doing it and thus the next try will be the right one."
-George F. Nordenholt

"There is no other solution to a man's problems but the day's honest work, the day's honest decisions, the day's generous utterance, and day's good deed."

- Clare Boothe Luce

"Every problem contains the seeds of its own solution. When you can't
solve the problem, manage it."
- Dr. Robert H. Schuller

"The block of granite, which was an obstacle in the path of the weak,
becomes a stepping stone in the path of the strong."
- Thomas Carlyle

"Real difficulties can be overcome, it is only the imaginary ones that
are unconquerable."
- Theodore N. Vail

"Many a man curses the rain that falls upon his head, and knows not
that it brings abundance to drive away hunger."
- Saint Basil

"Times of general calamity and confusion have ever been productive of
the greatest minds. The purest ore is produced from the hottest furnace,
and the brightest thunderbolt is elicited from the darkest storms."
- Charles Caleb Colton

"What is difficulty? Only a word indicating the degree of strength
requisite for accomplishing particular objects; a mere notice of the
necessary for exertion . . . mere stimulus to men."
- Samuel Warren

"We must look for the opportunity in every difficulty, instead of being
paralyzed at the thought of the difficulty in every opportunity."
- Walter E. Cole

"I used to believe that marriage would diminish me, reduce my options.
That you had to be someone less to live with someone else when, of
course, you have to be someone more."
- Candice Bergen

...man mind prefers to be spoon-fed with the thoughts of others,
...rived of such nourishment it will, reluctantly, begin to think for
...and such thinking, remember, is original thinking and may have
...e results."
...a Christie

...ve to, as you say, take a stand, do something toward shaking up
...tem . . . despair . . . is too easy an out."
...Marshall

...he unhappiness in life comes from people being afraid to go
...at things."
...m J. Lock

...rk of man is as the swimmer's: a vast ocean threatens to devour
...he front it not bravely, it will keep its word."
...as Carlyle

...leads nowhere except to more hiding."
...ret A. Robinson

...is no movement without our own resistance."
...ura Schlessinger

...oblems become smaller if you don't dodge them, but confront
..."
...m F. Halsey

...st way out of a problem is through it."
...ymous

...first woman God ever made was strong enough to turn the world
...down, these women together ought to able to turn it right side up
..."
...rner Truth

"We must prepare and study truth under every aspect, endeavoring to ignore nothing, if we do not wish to fall into the abyss of the unknown when the hour shall strike."
- *Marie von Ebner-Eschenbach*

"Life is the acceptance of responsibilities or their evasion; it is a business of meeting obligations or avoiding them. To every man the choice is continually being offered, and by the manner of his choosing you may fairly measure him."
 - *Ben Ames Williams*

"The superior man makes the difficulties to be overcome his first interests; success comes only later."
 - *Confucius*

"No man will succeed unless he is ready to face and overcome difficulties and is prepared to assume responsibilities."
- *William J. H. Boetcker*

"The harder the conflict, the more glorious the triumph. What we obtain too cheap, we esteem too lightly; 'tis dearness only that gives everything its value."
- *Thomas Paine*

"The greater the difficulty, the more glory in surmounting it."
- *Epicurus*

"Life affords no higher pleasure than that of surmounting difficulties."

- *Samuel Johnson*

"Can it be that man is essentially a being who loves to conquer difficulties, a creature whose function is to solve problems"
- *Gorham Munson*

"Conquering any difficulty always gives one a secret joy, for it means pushing back a boundary-line and adding to one's liberty."

- Henri Frederick Amiel

"To overcome difficulties is to experience the full delight of existence."
- Arthur Schopenhauer

"Success is to be measured not so much by the position that one has reached in life as by the obstacles he has overcome trying to succeed."
- Booker T. Washington

ADVERSITY

"Of course your life is valuable. It is invaluable. It was not obtained without intense suffering. The journey of the sperm to the egg is beset with difficulty. It is a tortuous journey. While many sperm are killed, many just give up and die. Their tragic end, lying dead in the middle passage, serves as a lesson to us that we cannot even come into existence without overcoming difficulty, since each and every one of us represents the resolve of a tiny sperm who overcame difficulty. Gold, Oil, Uranium, Diamonds, are valuable to us. They are in the ground. There is tremendous difficulty involved in getting them out of the ground before we can benefit from their value. Marriage is the desire to unite. The marriage vow is the statement of intention to unite. Immediately thereafter, difficulties arise. The difficulties are generated by our desire to unite in that they bring the man and woman together in a trying situation. Because while God created man and woman to incline toward one another and to seek unity with one another, He also made it a difficult thing to do. The process of uniting through marriage is a replication of the process of uniting with God. If we run away from the difficulties of marriage, we diminish our ability to face the difficulties of seeking to become one with Allah (God). Why do people get divorced? Why do people join an organization to unite, only to leave?"
- *Honorable Minister Louis Farrakhan*
Self-Improvement is the Basis for Community Development
Study Guide 3, Overcoming Difficulty

"Breakdowns can create breakthroughs. Things fall apart so things can fall together."
 - *Anonymous*

"The ultimate measure of a man is not where he stands in moments of comfort and convenience, but where he stands at times of challenge and controversy."
 - *Martin Luther King Jr.*

"Life is a series of experiences, each one of which makes us bigger, even though sometimes it is hard to realize this. For the world was built

to develop character, and we must learn that the setbacks and grieves which we endure help us in our marching onward."
- *Henry Ford*

"The difference between stumbling blocks and stepping stones is how you use them."
- *Anonymous*

"Not everything which is bad comes to hurt us."
- *Italian proverb*

"I love those who can smile in trouble, who can gather strength from distress, and grow brave by reflection. 'Tis the business of little minds to shrink, but they whose heart is firm, and whose conscience approves their conduct, will pursue their principles unto death."
- *Thomas Paine*

"A smooth sea never made a skillful mariner."
- *English proverb*

"Adversity has the effect of eliciting talents, which in prosperous circumstances would have lain dormant."
- *Horace*

"No one would ever have crossed the ocean if he could have gotten off the ship in a storm."
- *Unknown* Source

"Frogs have it easy, they can eat what bugs them."
- *Anonymous*

"There will be no crown bearers in heaven who are not cross bearers on earth."
- *Anonymous*

"A stumble may prevent a fall."
- *English proverb*

"Adversity has the same effect on a man that severe training has on the pugilist -- it reduces him to his fighting weight."
- *Josh Billings*

"Adversity is the first path to truth."
- *Lord Byron*

"Every adversity, every failure, every heartache carries with it the seed of an equal or greater benefit."
- *Napoleon Hill*

"As a rule, adversity reveals genius and prosperity hides it."
- *Horace*

"The worst thing that happens to you may be the best thing for you if you don't let it get the best of you."
- *Will Rogers*

"Brave men rejoice in adversity, just as brave soldiers triumph in war."
- *Lucius Annaeus Seneca*

"The bravest sight in the world is to see a great man struggling against adversity."
- *Lucius Annaeus Seneca*

"Cushion the painful effects of hard blows by keeping the enthusiasm going strong, even if doing so requires struggle."
- *Norman Vincent Peale*

"Those who aim at great deeds must also suffer greatly."
- *Plutarch*

"Affliction comes to us, not to make us sad but sober; not to make us sorry but wise."
- *Henry Ward Beecher*

...ps are like knives, that either serve us or cut us, as we grasp
... the blade or by the handle."
... Russell Lowell

...o knows the darkness shall learn to live in the light."
...mous

...ars are constantly shining, but often we do not see them until the
... urs."
...ymous

...'t know I'd have to be torn down before I could be built up."

...mous

... going is real easy, beware, you may be headed down hill and
... ow it."
...mous

... the gift for employing all the vicissitudes of life to one's own
... ge and to that of one's craft that a large part of genius consists."

... C. Lichtenberg

... many who are struggling against adversity who are happy, and
... though abounding in wealth, who are wretched."

...s Cornelius Tacitus

... the test of gold; adversity, of strong men."
... Annaeus Seneca

...lure is the first thing that a child ought to learn, and that which he
... e the most need to know."
... Jacques Rousseau

...sity is the state in which man mostly easily becomes acquainted
... mself, being especially free of admirers then."

- Samuel Johnson

"He knows not his own strength that hath not met adversity."
- Ben Jonson

"What is to give light must endure the burning."
- Viktor Frankl

"March on. Do not tarry. To go forward is to move toward perfection.
March on, and fear not the thorns, or the sharp stones on life's path."
- Kahlil Gibran

"Prosperity is a great teacher; adversity is a greater. Possession pampers
the mind; privation trains and strengthens it."
- William Hazlitt

"One sees great things from the valley; only small things from the peak."

- Gilbert Keith Chesterton

"The actual tragedies of life bear no relation to one's preconceived ideas.
In the event, one is always bewildered by their simplicity, their grandeur
of design, and by that element of the bizarre which seems inherent in
them."
- Jean Cocteau

"A man is a god in ruins."
- Ralph Waldo Emerson

"Prosperity is not without many fears and distastes; adversity not
without many comforts and hopes."
- Francis Bacon

"We are always on the anvil; by trials God is shaping us for higher
things."
- Henry Ward Beecher

"I'm not afraid of storms, for I'm learning to sail my ship."

- Louisa May Alcott

"Problems are only opportunities in work clothes."
- Henry J. Kaiser

"Great spirits have always encountered violent opposition from mediocre minds."
- Albert Einstein

"Without a struggle, there can be no progress."
- Frederick Douglass

"A wise man adapts himself to circumstances as water shapes itself to the vessel that contains it."
- Chinese proverb

"In the midst of winter, I found there was within me an invincible summer."
- Albert Careb

"Times of great calamity and confusion have ever been productive of the greatest minds. The purest ore is produced from the hottest furnace, and the brightest thunderbolt is elicited from the darkest storm." - *Charles Caleb Colton*

"Difficulties strengthen the mind, as well as labor does the body." - *Luscius Annaeus Seneca*

"A friend loveth at all times, and a brother is born for adversity." - *Proverbs 17:17*

"Adversity is the trial of principle. Without it a man hardly knows whether he is honest or not."
- Henry Fielding

"Always seek out the seed of triumph in every adversity."
- Og Mandino

"Education is an ornament in prosperity and a refuge in adversity."
- *Aristotle*

"Fresh activity is the only means of overcoming adversity."
- *Johann Wolfgang von Goethe*

"In prosperity, our friends know us; in adversity, we know our friends."
- *John Churton Collins*

"In times of great stress or adversity, it's always best to keep busy, to plow your anger and your energy into something positive."
- *Lee Iacocca*

"Many who seem to be struggling with adversity are happy; many, amid great affluence, are utterly miserable."
- *Tacitus*

"One who gains strength by overcoming obstacles possesses the only strength which can overcome adversity."
- *Albert Schweitzer*

"Prosperity makes friends, adversity tries them."
- *Publilius Syrus*

"Show me someone who has done something worthwhile, and I'll show you someone who has overcome adversity."
- *Lou Holtz*

"Test a servant while in the discharge of his duty, a relative in difficulty, a friend in adversity, and a wife in misfortune."
- *Chanakya*

"The firmest of friendships have been formed in mutual adversity, as iron is most strongly united by the fiercest flame."
- *Charles Caleb Colton*

"The friend in my adversity I shall always cherish most. I can better trust those who helped to relieve the gloom of my dark hours than those who are so ready to enjoy with me the sunshine of my prosperity."
- *Ulysses S. Grant*

"There is in every true woman's heart, a spark of heavenly fire, which lies dormant in the broad daylight of prosperity, but which kindles up and beams and blazes in the dark hour of adversity."
- *Washington Irving*

"Three hundred years ago a prisoner condemned to the Tower of London carved on the wall of his cell this sentiment to keep up his spirits during his long imprisonment: 'It is not adversity that kills, but the impatience with which we bear adversity."
- *James Keller*

"True friendship is a plant of slow growth, and must undergo and withstand the shocks of adversity, before it is entitled to the appellation."
- *George Washington*

"Very often out of adversity that's when the best work comes."
- *Tom Cochrane*

"Age wrinkles the body. Quitting wrinkles the soul."
- *Douglas MacArthur*

"Pain is temporary. It may last a minute, or an hour, or a day, or a year, but eventually it will subside and something else will take its place. If I quit, however, it lasts forever."
- *Lance Armstrong*

"Prosperity discovers vice, adversity discovers virtue."
- *Sir Francis Bacon*

"The best way out is always through."
- *Robert Frost*

"Remember, no one can make you feel inferior without your consent."
- *Eleanor Roosevelt*

"Watch your thoughts; they become words. Watch your words; they become actions. Watch your actions; they become habits. Watch your habits; they become character. Watch your character; it becomes your destiny."
- *Frank Outlaw*

"Love is much more fundamental than any kind of thinking or believing. It is the root and basis of who you are, at the most fundamental level. This means that anything other than love as an expression of your being is artificial and unnatural and is a result of not knowing who you are."
- *Bill Harris*

"Money doesn't bring happiness and creativity. Your creativity and happiness brings money."
- *Sam Rosen*

"A truth's initial commotion is directly proportional to how deeply the lie was believed . . . When a well-packaged web of lies has been sold gradually to the masses over generations, the truth will seem utterly preposterous and its speaker, a raving lunatic."
- *Dresden James*

"Tell me and I'll forget. Show me and I'll remember. Involve me and I'll understand."
- *Confucius*

"Nearly all men can stand adversity, but if you want to test a man's character, give him power."
- *Abraham Lincoln*

"Gratitude unlocks the fullness of life. It turns what we have into enough, and more. It turns denial into acceptance, chaos to order, confusion to clarity. It can turn a meal into a feast, a house into a home,

...er into a friend. Gratitude makes sense of our past, brings peace
...y, and creates a vision for tomorrow."
...ly *Beattie*

...ar that we are inadequate, but our deepest fear is that we are
...ul beyond measure. It is our light, not our darkness, that most
...is us. We ask ourselves: "Who am I to be brilliant, gorgeous,
...d, fabulous?" Actually, who are you not to be these things? You
...ild of God. Your playing small doesn't serve the world. There is
...g enlightening about shrinking so that other people around you
...eel insecure. We are all meant to shine as children do. We are
...manifest the glory of God that is within us. It is not just in
...f us; it is in everyone. And as we let our light shine, we
...iously give other people permission to do the same. As we are
...d from our own fear, our presence automatically releases

...nne *Williamson*

...ing is not enough; we must apply. Willing is not enough; we
...do."
...n von *Goethe*

...sm is something we can avoid easily - by saying nothing, doing
...g, and being nothing."
...tle

...come to the frightening conclusion that I am the decisive
...t. It is my personal approach that creates the climate. It is my
...ood that makes the weather. I possess tremendous power to
...fe miserable or joyous. I can be a tool of torture or an
...ment of inspiration. I can humiliate or humor, hurt or heal. In all
...ns, it is my response that decides whether a crisis is escalated or
...ated, and a person is humanized or de-humanized. If we treat
...as they are, we make them worse. If we treat people as they
...o be, we help them become what they are capable of becoming."
...ne

...ill become visible as God's image is reborn in you."

- St. Bernard of Clairveux

"A coward gets scared and quits. A hero gets scared, but still goes on."
- Anonymous

"The best thing parents can do for their children is to love each other."
 - Anonymous

"In the midst of great joy, do not promise anyone anything. In the midst of great anger, do not answer anyone's letter."
- Chinese proverb

"Deal with the faults of others as gently as with your own."
- Chinese proverb

"Problems cannot be solved at the same level of awareness that created them."
- Albert Einstein

"Expecting life to treat you well because you are a good person is like expecting an angry bull not to charge because you are a vegetarian."
- Shari R. Barr

"Comfort is found among those who agree with you; growth among those who don't."
- Anonymous

"If you can find a path with no obstacles, it probably doesn't lead anywhere."
- Frank A. Clark

"Persistence. Nothing in the world can take the place of persistence. Talent will not; nothing is more common than unsuccessful men with talent. Genius will not; unrewarded genius is almost a proverb. Education will not; the world is full of educated derelicts. Persistence and determination alone are omnipotent. The slogan, 'Press on,' has solved and always will solve the problems of the human race."
- U.S. President Calvin Coolidge

"It's easy to be brave from a safe distance."
- *Aesop*

"The pessimist sees difficulty in every opportunity. The optimist sees opportunity in every difficulty."
- *Winston Churchill*

"When inquiry is suppressed by previous knowledge, or by the authority and experience of another, then learning becomes mere imitation, and imitation causes a human being to repeat what is learned without experiencing it."
- *J. Krishnamurti*

"If you really want to do something, you'll find a way; if you don't, you'll find an excuse."
- *Anonymous*

"Your children are not your children. They are the sons and daughters of Life's longing for itself. They come through you but not from you, and though they are with you, yet they belong not to you. You may give them your love, but not your thoughts. For they have their own thoughts. You may house their bodies but not their souls, for their souls dwell in the house of tomorrow, which you cannot visit, not even in your dreams. You may strive to be like them, but seek not to make them like you. For life goes not backward, nor tarries with yesterday."
- *Kahlil Gibran*

"Difficulties should act as a tonic. They should spur us to greater exertion."
- *B.C. Forbes*

"There are times in everyone's life when something constructive is born out of adversity . . . when things seem so bad that you've got to grapy or fate by the shoulders and shake it."
- *Anonymous*

"Brave men rejoice in adversity, just as brave soldiers triumph in war."
- *Marcus Annaeus Seneca*

"Some minds seem almost to create themselves, springing up under every disadvantage and working their solitary but irresistible way through a thousand obstacles."
-*Washington Irving*

"If you will call your troubles experiences, and remember that every experience develops some latent force within you, you will grow vigorous and happy, however adverse your circumstances may seem to be."
 - *John Heywood*

"People wish to be settled; only as far as they are unsettled is there any hope for them."
- *Ralph Waldo Emerson*

"Difficulties are meant to rouse, not discourage. The human spirit is to grow strong by conflict."
- *William Ellery Channing*

"Adversity causes some men to break, others to break records."
- *William A. Ward*

"The thought that we are enduring the unendurable is one of the things that keeps us going."
- *Molly Haskell*

"A certain amount of opposition is a great help to a man; it is what he wants and must have to be good for anything. Hardship and opposition are the native soil of manhood and self-reliance."
- *John Neal*

"Without the burden of afflictions it is impossible to reach the height of grace. The gift of grace increases as the struggles increase."
- *Saint Rose of Lima*

"The effects of opposition are wonderful. There are men who rise refreshed on hearing of a threat, men to whom a crisis, which intimidates and paralyzes the majority, comes as graceful and beloved as a bride!"
- Ralph Waldo Emerson

"He that wrestles with us strengthens our nerves and sharpens our skills. Our antagonist is our helper."
 - Edmond Burke

"The block of granite which was an obstacle in the path of the weak becomes a steppingstone in the path of the strong."
- Thomas Carlyle

"Strong people are made by opposition, like kites that go up against the wind."
 - Frank Harris

"Men strive for peace, but it is their enemies that give them strength, and I think if man no longer had enemies, he would have to invent them, for his strength only grows from struggle."
- Louis L'Amour

"Enemies can be incentive to survive and become someone in spite of them. Enemies can keep you alert and aware."
- Louis L'Amour

"Problems are the cutting edge that distinguishes between success and failure. Problems . . . create our courage and wisdom."
- M. Scott Peek

"It is often better to have a great deal of harm happen to one than a little; a great deal may rouse you to remove what a little will only accustom you to endure."
- Grenville Kleiser

"The world is a wheel always turning," philosophized Mrs. Pelz. "Those who were high go down low, and those who've been low go up higher."
 - *Anzia Yezierska*

"There is often in people to whom 'the worst' has happened an almost transcendent freedom, for they have faced 'the worst' and survived it."
- *Carol Pearson*

"Out of suffering have emerged the strongest souls; the most massive characters are seared with scars."
- *Edwin H. Chapin*

"Don't look forward to the day when you stop suffering. Because when it comes, you'll know you're dead."
- *Tennessee Williams*

"How sublime a thing it is to suffer and be strong."
- *Henry Wadsworth Longfellow*

"Character cannot be developed in ease and quiet. Only through experience of trail and suffering can the soul be strengthened, vision cleared, ambition inspired, and success achieved."
- *Helen Keller*

"Never to suffer would have been never to have been blessed."
- *Edgar Allan Poe*

"It is somehow reassuring to discover that the word 'travel' is derived from "travail," denoting the pains of childbirth."
- *Jessica Mitford*

"True knowledge comes only through suffering."
- *Elizabeth Barrett Browning*

"Suffering raises up those souls that are truly great; it is only small souls that are made mean-spirited by it."
 - *Alexandra David-Neel*

ints rejoiced at injuries and persecutions, because in forgiving
ey had something to present to God when they prayed to Him."
of Avila

he discontent of man, the world's best progress springs."
Wheeler Wilcox

lifficulties and struggles of today are but the price we must pay
accomplishments and victories of tomorrow."
J.H. Boetcker

ence may be hard but we claim its gifts because they are real,
ough our feet bleed on its stones."
Parker Follett

n, no palm, no thorns, no throne; no gall, no glory; no cross, no

Penn

of stress and difficulty are seasons of opportunity when the
progress are sown."
F. Woodlock

m cannot be polished without friction, nor man perfected
trails."
cius

complain about your troubles; they are responsible for more
lf of your income."
R. Updegraff

lem is a chance for you to do your best."
Ellington

cret of a leader lies in the tests he has faced over the whole
of his life and the habit of action he develops in meeting those

- Gail Sheehy

"Times of general calamity and confusion have been productive of the greatest minds. The purist ore is produced from the hottest furnace, and the brightest thunderbolt is elicited from the darkest storms."
- Charles Caleb Colton

"The habits of a vigorous mind are formed contending with difficulties."
 - Abigail Adams

"A diamond is a chunk of coal that made good under pressure."
-Anonymous

"Unless a man has been kicked around a little, you can't really depend upon him to amount to anything."
 - William Feather

"If you have to be careful because of oppression and censorship, this pressure produces diamonds."
-Tatyana Tolstaya

"Adversity is another way to measure the greatness of individuals. I never had a crisis that didn't make me stronger."
- Lou Holtz

"A difficult childhood gave me] a kind of cocky confidence . . . I could never have so little that I hadn't had less. It took away my fear."
 - Jacqueline Cochran

"Supporting myself at an early age was the best training for my life I could have possibly received."
- Lea Thompson

"I would never have amounted to anything were it not for adversity. I was forced to come up the hard way."
- J.C. Penney

"Adversity introduces man to himself."
- *Anonymous*

"I thank God for my handicaps for, through them, I have found myself, my work, and my God."
- *Helen Keller*

"This struggle of people against their conditions, this is where you find the meaning in life."
- *Rose Chernin*

"Adversity has ever been considered as the state in which a man most easily becomes acquainted with himself, being free from flatterers."
- *Samuel Johnson*

"In all things preserve integrity; and the consciousness of thine own uprightness will alleviate the toil of business, soften the disappointments, and give thee an humble confidence before God, when the ingratitude of man, or the times may rob thee of other rewards."
- *Barbara Paley*

"He knows not his own strength who hath not met adversity."
- *Samuel Johnson*

"In the depth of winter, I finally learned that there was in me an invincible summer."
- *Albert Camus*

"Adversity is the trail of principle. Without it a man hardly knows whether he is honest or not."
- *Henry Fielding*

"I think the years I have spent in prison have been the most formative and important in my life because of the discipline, the sensations, but chiefly the opportunity to think clearly, to try to understand things."

- *Jawaharlal Nehru*

"Difficulties are things that show what men are."
- *Epictetus*

"Disappointment is the nurse of wisdom."
- *Sir Bayle Roche*

"Challenges make you discover things about yourself that you never really knew. They're what make the instrument stretch, what make you go beyond the norm."
- *Cicely Tyson*

"Adversity has the effect of eliciting talents, which, in prosperous circumstances, would have lain dormant."
- *Horace*

"When a man is pushed, tormented, defeated, he has a chance to learn something; he has been put on his wits . . . he had gained facts, learned his ignorance, is cured of the insanity of conceit, has got moderation and real skill."
- *Ralph Waldo Emerson*

"From their errors and mistakes, the wise and good learn wisdom for the future."
- *Plutarch*

"Adversity reveals genius, prosperity conceals it."
- *Horace*

"Hope begins in the dark, the stubborn hope that if you just show up and try to do the right thing, the dawn will come. You wait and watch and work; you don't give up."
- *Anne Lamott*

"All sorts of spiritual gifts come through privations, if they are accepted."
- *Janet Erskine Stuart*

"God will not look you over for medals, degrees or diplomas, but for scars."
- *Anonymous*

"He who serves God with what costs him nothing, will do very little service, you may depend on it."
 - *Susan Warner*

"Sorrow has its reward. It never leaves us where it found us."
- *Mary Baker Eddy*

"The same reason makes a man a religious enthusiast that makes a man an enthusiast any other way: an uncomfortable mind in an uncomfortable body."
- *William Hazlitt*

"Who has never tasted what is bitter does not know what is sweet."
- *German proverb*

"Victory is sweetest when you've known defeat."
- *Malcolm Forbes*

"No man better knows what good is then he who has endured evil."
- *Anonymous*

"If you want the rainbow, you gotta put up with the rain."
- Dolly Parton

"He that can't endure the bad will not live to see the good."
- *Yiddish proverb*

"If you will call your troubles experiences' and remember that every experience develops some latent force within you, you will grow vigorous and happy, however adverse your circumstances may seem to be."
 - *John Heywoodr*

"Anything other than death is a minor injury."

- Bill Muncey

"The most valuable gift I ever received was the gift of insecurity my father left us. My mother's love might not have prepared me for life the way my father's departure did. He forced us out on the road, where we had to ear our bread."
- Lillian Gish

"When written in Chinese, the word "crisis" is composed of two characters. One represents danger, and the other represents opportunity."
- John F. Kennedy

"Our real blessings often appear to us in the shape of pains, losses and disappointments; but let us have patience, and we soon shall see them in their proper figures."
- Joseph Addison

"To every disadvantage there is a corresponding advantage."
- W. Clement Stone

"Diseases can be out spiritual flat tires - disruptions in our lives that seem to be disasters at the time, but end by redirecting our lives in a meaningful way."
- Bernie S. Siegel, M.D.

"Our way is not soft grass; it's a mountain path with lots of rocks. But it goes upwards, forward, toward the sun."
- Dr. Ruth Wertheimer

"Failure is, in a sense, the highway to success, inasmuch as every discovery of what is false leads us to seek earnestly after what is true, and very fresh experience points out some form of error which we shall afterward carefully avoid."
- John Keats

"Although the world is full of suffering; it is also full of the overcoming of it."

... Keller

... not be needlessly bitter; certain failures are sometimes fruitful."
... Coiran

... are the uses of adversity."
... Shakespeare

... th does not come from winning. Your struggles develop your
... hs. When you go through hardships and decide not to surrender,
... trength."
... Schwarzenegger

... ltimate measure of a man is not where he stands in moments of
... and convenience, but where he stands at times of challenge and
... ersy."
... Luther King Jr.

... free a camel of the burden of his hump; you may be freeing him
... ing a camel."
... Chesterton

... firmer and move secure up hill than down."
... l de Montaigne

... irtue of adversity is fortitude, which in mortals is the heroical
... "
... is Bacon

... n an obstacle to one's advantage is a great step towards victory."
... h proverb

... occasions do not make heroes or cowards; they simply unveil
... the eyes of men . . . crisis shows us what we have become."   -
... Westcott

... hristian ideal has not been tried and found wanting. It has been
... difficult and left untried."

- G.K.Chesterton

A PRAYER

I asked for strength and God gave me difficulties to make me strong. I asked for wisdom and God gave me problems to solve. I asked for prosperity and God gave me brawn and brains to work. I asked for courage and God gave me dangers to overcome. I asked for patience and God placed me in situations where I was forced to wait. I asked for love and God gave me troubled people to help. I asked for favors and God gave me opportunities. I received nothing I wanted I received everything I needed. *MY PRAYER HAS BEEN ANSWERED.*

THE DILEMMA

To laugh is to risk appearing a fool. To weep is to risk appearing sentimental. To reach out for another is to risk involvement. To expose feelings is to risk rejection. To place your dreams before a crowd is to risk ridicule. To love is to risk not being loved in return. To go forward in the face of overwhelming odds is to risk failure. But risks must be taken because the greatest hazard in life is to risk nothing. The person who risks nothing does nothing, has nothing, is nothing. He may avoid suffering and sorrows, but he cannot learn, feel, change, grow, or love. Chained by his certitudes, he is a slave - he has forfeited his freedom.

-Anonymous

HIP-HOP INSPIRATIONAL LYRICS

"Who are you? I want to encourage you to be the light that produces a revolution. That word sometimes inspires fear, but we shouldn't be afraid. Jesus was the supreme revolutionary. Revolution means a complete change that brings a thing back to its original point . . . Who are you? You are the bearers of light or darkness. If you continue to make your people think that the way we act is right, then you are an emissary of darkness and not a bearer or light. The artists are the most important people. You are the teachers."

- Honorable Minister Louis Farrakhan
The Evolution of Hip Hop
October 14, 2007

Eminem (8 Mile)
I'm a man, gotta make a new plan
Time for me to just stand up and travel new land
Time for me to just take matters into my own hands
Once I'm over these tracks man, I'ma never look back.

Ludacris (Grew Up a Screw Up)
When I came into the game
They ain't do nothing but doubt me
Now the whole game's changed
And it ain't nothing without me.

The Roots (Sacrifice)
Sometimes before you smile you got to cry
You need a heart that's filled with music
If you use it you can fly.

Mos Def (Sunshine)
I give a @#*! about what brand you are
I'm concerned what type of man you are
What your principles and standards are.

Kanye West (Bring Me Down feat. Brandy)

They gon' have to take my life 'fore they take my drive
'Cause when I was barely living, that's what kept me alive
Just the thought that maybe it could be
Better than where we at at this time
Make it out of this grind, 'fore I'm out of my mind.

Kanye West (Big Brother)
If you admire somebody you should go ahead and tell 'em
People never get the flowers while they can still smell 'em

Fabolous (Change Up)
Being broke is a joke, I never found it funny
That's why I count my blessings
As much as I count my money.

Reflection Eternal (Memories Live)
Tap into your chi, utilize your memory
To help you see clearly, then get back to me
Actually, nothing's new under the sun
So when life be stressing me
My remedy is bringing back sweet memories

Dilated Peoples (No Retreat feat. B-Real)
Stand my ground, dig in with both feet
No surrender, no turning no cheek, no retreat

Murs (Yesterday & Today)
Yesterday I felt the most hated
I thought I couldn't take it, they said I couldn't make it
And today I'm feeling brand new
I got nothing to lose, I'm about to make moves.

A Tribe Called Quest (Stressed Out)
I swallowed my pride and let that nonsense ride
Because I'm positive, it seems that negative died.

Elohin (Higher feat. Ken Nether)
No longer dreaming, like I'm sleep in a coma
Success in the air, I can sniff the aroma
A life of mistakes had to face it and own up
I thought like a kid, now your boy is a grown up
Uh, been through the fire feeling heat like a sauna
If faith was a number, hope I'm meeting my quota
Hope I pass the test and get the diploma
Life is full of lemons I don't need the corona.

Mystic (The Life feat. Kam, Talib Kweli)
Tried to call, or at least beep the Lord
But didn't have a touch-tone
It's a dog-eat-dog world, you gotta mush on

Black Star (Respiration)
My advice is to know your worth, everyday go to work
Hold up your people till your shoulders hurt.

A Tribe Called Quest (Stressed Out)
I really know how it feels to be, stressed out, stressed out
When you're face to face with your adversity
I really know how it feels to be, stressed out, stressed out
We're gonna make this thing work out eventually.

Black Star (K.O.S.)
The most important time in history is now, the present
So count your blessings, cause time can't define the essence.

The Roots (Glitches)
The big picture's the focus
@#*! being hopeless.

Binary Star (I Know Why The Caged Bird Sings)
I studied my thoughts, my ways, the routes I took
Though I read daily, it ain't all about the books
It's all about the lessons you learn, through your experience
Applying it in a positive way, period.

Lupe Fiasco (Words I never Said)
I think that all the silence, is worse than all violence
Fear is such a weak emotion, that's why I despise it
We're scared of almost everything, afraid to even tell the truth
So scared of what you think of me, I'm scared of even telling you
Sometimes I'm like the only person I feel safe to tell it to
I'm locked inside a cell in me, I know that there's a jail in you
Consider this your bailing out, so take a breath inhale a few
My screams is finally gettin' free, my thoughts is finally yellin' through.

Eminem (Lose Yourself)
So here I go, it's my shot, feet fail me not
This may be the only opportunity that I got.

50 Cent (Many Men)
Sunny days wouldn't be special, if it wasn't for rain
Joy wouldn't feel so good, if it wasn't for pain.

Immortal Technique (Caught In The Hustle)
If the solution has never been to look in yourself
How is it that you expect to find it anywhere else?

Fabolous (It's My Time feat. Jeremih)
Go hard today
Can't worry 'bout the past
'Cause that was yesterday
I'ma put it on tonight
'Cause it's my time.

Foreign Exchange (All That You Are)
Solved it – my blood fam on the bandwagon
Can't believe the man put his plan into action
They rather that I choose a different plan for my passion
Couldn't understand, I demand satisfaction.

weli (Gutter Rainbows)
n't fashion rap, I'm bringin' the passion back
where the trouble at, that's my natural habitat
o!) I take it with me in the booth
livin' we owe respect, to the dead we only owe the truth.

m (It's A New Day)
asleep last night, tired from the fight
en fighting for tomorrow, all my life
oke up this morning, feeling brand new
the dream that I've been dreaming
ally came true.

is (Mouths to Feed)
onster in this game, I turn 20 into 50
hundred and a hundred to a Bentley
ley to a building and a building to a 'scraper
eep up with the news but I get that daily paper.

aliph (Physics 720 and the Universal Laws of...)
p building, and hate love that loves hate
ow the world that Neo ain't
y way out the Matrix
ed if you believe to achieve, then you'll make it.

li (Soundtrack to my Life)
some issues that nobody can see
of these emotions are pourin' outta me
them to the light for you
right this is the soundtrack to my life.

5 (Great Expectations)
am slash career appears ever so clear
m able to touch, smell, feel, speak, and hear
s cheer, my time is finally here
t depart the present cause the future is near.

Young Jeezy (The Inspiration)
Got the weight of the world on my shoulders
And I swear it feels like ten thousand boulders
And it's so heavy, but I'm so ready
Feels like I was born for this.

The Roots (Glitches)
Out in the world, up against tremendous odds
Some will let it break 'em and throw in they cards
But my squad remains focused when we goin' for ours.

Kayne West (Amazing)
And no matter what
You'll never take that from me
My reign is as far as your eyes can see
It's amazing, so amazing.

Fabolous (Change Up)
Money can't buy happiness
But it's a damn good down payment.

Blackalicious (Release)
Motivate, accelerate, never wait
Know your weight, throw away hate
Grow and make weight of your older dates
Elevate, concentrate, get your focus straight
And orchestrate fate
Just motivate, accelerate, never wait
Show the way, no escape
Take hold and shift shape, live a longer day.

Self Made (Wale feat. Rick Ross)
If I woke up tomorrow and didn't have a dolla
As long as I have my heart, I can get it all over.

The Diplomats (More Than Music)
I put my life on paper when I record my music
You can look me in my eyes and see it's more than music.

K'Naan (Wavin' Flag)
Born to a throne, stronger than Rome
But violent prone, poor people zone
But it's my home, all I have known
Where I got grown, streets we would roam
Out of the darkness, I came the farthest
Among the hardest survival
Learn from these streets, it can be bleak
Except no defeat, surrender, retreat.

Brother Ali (The Puzzle)
Listen, when life leaves you beaten up
Don't lay around in it, hurry pick them pieces up.

Kidz In The Hall (Take Over The World)
What you're about to do is so historic,
They can't deny the win, if you keep scorin'
Whatever's in your heart, don't ignore it
And if you doubt yourself, sing this chorus:
So close your eyes, for though you dream
And keep your head to the sky
When times get rough, and the clouds get dark,
And you need to ask yourself why
Just listen to the words I say, you'll find a way
To keep pushin' to get by
And if you keep this on your mind, stay on your grind
It'll be your time, to take over the world.

Kanye West (The Good Life)
50 told me go 'head switch the style up
And if they hate then let 'em hate
And watch the money pile up.

Tupac (Keep Ya Head Up)
And since we all came from a woman
Got our name from a woman and our game from a woman
I wonder why we take from our women
Why we rape our women, do we hate our women?
I think it's time to kill for our women
Time to heal our women, be real to our women
And if we don't we'll have a race of babies
That will hate the ladies, that make the babies
And since a man can't make one
He has no right to tell a woman when and where to create one
So will the real men get up
I know you're fed up, ladies, but keep your head up.

People Under the Stairs (Acid Raindrops)
Let the problems in your mind become ancient artifacts
Perhaps these raps can help you alleviate
The things that's got you trippin', yo watch me demonstrate
First you ignore the nonsense and clear your conscience
Let your pen touch the paper write verbs and consonants
As the words become a sentence you start to feelin' different
The stress is out your mind you feel like the weight was lifted.

DMX (Do You)
For two years keep it real, hold back all tears, face your fears
Become a man before your time
Rap, but live out your rhymes
Let 'em know what's on your mind, then you'll get your shine
In time, everything you hear will come true
But you won't be doin' me, you'll be doin' you.

Murs (Dreamchasers)
We all chase money 'cause
We're scared to chase dreams.

Immortal Technique (Leaving the Past)
I refuse to be concerned with condescending advice
'Cause I'm the only @#*! that can change my life.

Murs (Yesterday & Today)
Nobody's perfect, ain't none of us worthless
We all got a place, and we all got a purpose.

Gang Starr (No More Mr. Nice Guy)
Continue on with my journey
All the negative ones don't concern me
My eyes are wise, I got cause to live
Positive, have to give, every way
Every day of my life, so I fight for the right
And get hype, so heed what I feed
And get fed, then you'll be livin' two steps ahead.

Lil' Flip (What I Been Through)
It's time to be a man, time to make a plan
It's cool to make a hundred, but it's best to make a grand.

Black Star (Thieves in the Night)
I give a damn if any fan recalls my legacy
I'm trying to live life in the sight of God's memory.

T.I. (No Matter What)
I ain't dead, I ain't done
I ain't scared, I ain't run
But still I stand.

Dead Prez (Happiness)
I put the great Mother Nature on a pedestal
She always fly, but today, she's exceptional
If I had a chance to make a wish
Every day would be just like this, full of happiness.

T.I. (Good Life)
I was born into poverty, raised in the sewage
Streets always be apart of me, they made me the truest
And even when my days were the bluest
Never ran from adversity, instead I ran to it

Fear ain't in the heart of me, I learned just do it
You get courage in your fears right after you go through it.

Blue Scholars (No Rest For The Weary)
Hold your head high soldier, it ain't over yet
That's why we call it a struggle
You're supposed to sweat.

T.I. (No Matter What)
All you can do is handle it, worst thing you can do is panic
Use it to your advantage, avoid insanity manage
To conquer, every obstacle, make impossible possible
Even when winning's illogical, losing is still far from optional.

Ludacris (Freedom of Preach)
When you open up your mouth, everything of God comes out
And it commands attention, it commands change
I'm talking about the power that's inside of you.

Drake (Light Up)
They always tell me nobody's workin' as hard as you
And even though I laugh it off, man, it's probably true
'Cause while my closest friends out there partying
I'm just here making all of the music that they party to.

Foreign Exchange (Connected)
I fell asleep with this beat on repeat
Repetitively, life seems to grip me
I'm trying to be a better man, please believe me
Ready and god willing if you ready to teach me.

Xzibit (Back 2 The Way It Was)
You can speculate, on every breath I take
But you can never ever take my place
I stay strong whether right or I'm wrong
Through the struggle I will live on.

Matter What)
ill take you to hell, just to get you to heaven
though it's heavy, the load I will carry.

rez (Hip Hop)
uld rather have a Lexus? or Justice?
n? Or some substance?
er? A necklace? Or freedom?

Peoples (Worst Comes to Worst)
is good, I got my peeps in the mix so
omes to worst my people come first.

us (Change Up)
the money, but don't let it make me
if I go broke…you couldn't break me.

ots (How I Got Over)
cried out cause I grew up cryin'
got a sales pitch I ain't buyin'
ryin' to convince me that I ain't tryin'
nspired
dmired
d and sick of being sick and tired
ing in the hood where the shots are fired
n' to live, so to live we dyin'
t like I am.

n (Be)
for the dawn to rise
nto my daughter's eyes
lize I'ma learn through her
ssiah might even return through her
do it I gotta change the world through her.

Del Tha Funkee Homosapien (Situations)
You can't let emotions control you
Fools will go and try to throw you
They know its a way to control you
They say I'm cold, but I told you
I've got goals, I focus on the whole view.

Eminem (It's OK)
One day I plan to be a family man happily married
I wanna grow to be so old that I have to be carried
Till I'm glad to be buried
And leave this crazy world
And have at least a half a million for my baby girl
It may be early to be planning this stuff
Cause I'm still struggling hard to be the man, and it's tough
Cause man it's been rough, but still I manage enough
I've been taken advantage of, damaged and scuffed
My hands have been cuffed
But I don't panic and huff, frantic and puff
Or plan to give up, the minute shit hits the fan it erupts
I'm anteing up double or nothing, I've been trouble enough
And I'm sick of struggling and suffering, see
My destiny's to rest at ease, till I'm impressed and pleased
With my progress, I won't settle for less than cheese
I'm on a quest to seize all, my own label to call
Way before my baby is able to crawl
I'm too stable to fall, the pressure motivates
To know I hold the weight of boulders on my shoulder blades.

Will.i.am (It's A New Day)
If you and I made it this far
Well then hey, we can make it all the way
And they said, "No, we can't," and we said, "Yes, we can"
Remember it's you, and me, together.

Black Star (K.O.S.)
At exactly which point do you start to realize
That life without knowledge is, death in disguise?

That's why Knowledge Of Self is like life after death
Apply it to your life, let destiny manifest.

Asher Roth (Sour Patch Kids)
Donate your dollars, raise a toddler
Help a mother, save a father
Cause poverty is probably our biggest problem
And it ain't gonna stop with Obama
To save the world we must start at the bottom.

Blackalicious (Deception)
If you're blessed with the talent, utilize it to the fullest
Be true to yourself and stay humble.

Rick Ross (Shot to the Heart)
Determined to be the best
Not looking back at regrets
How many people you bless
Is how you measure success.

T.I. (No Matter What)
I was born without a dime
Out the gutter I climbed
Spoke my mind and didn't stutter one time
Ali said even the greatest gotta suffer sometimes.

Young Jeezy (The Inspiration)
The big question is what can I do for the youth?
Everybody lyin' to 'em so I told 'em the truth.

The Notorious B.I.G. (Ready To Die)
Uh, damn right I like the life I live
'Cause I went from negative to positive.

Young Jeezy (Let's Get It / Sky's the Limit)
The world is yours and everything in it
It's out there, get on your grind and get it.

Maino (All of the Above feat. T-Pain)
I wave hi to the haters, mad that I finally made it
Take a look and you can tell that I'm destined for greatness.

Mystic (The Life feat. Kam, Talib Kweli)
This is for solemn prayers, that uplift the soul
And protect all people from the blistering cold
This is for soldiers and survivors, hustlers and the 9-to-5ers
Those who know the sting of being raised without a father
For those who know the beauty, that grows from pain
Who knows the burn of hot tea is a cleansing thang.

Successful (Drake)
I want it all, that's why I strive for it
Diss me and you'll never hear a reply for it
Any award show or party I get fly for it
I know that its comin'
I just hope that I'm alive for it.

Young Jeezy (The Inspiration)
Got the weight of the world on my shoulders
And I swear it feels like ten thousand boulders
And it's so heavy, but I'm so ready
Feels like I was born for this.

PARABLES

POEMS

Pleasure v. Sorrow
"I walked a mile with Pleasure
She chattered all the way;
But left me none the wiser
For all she had to say.
I walked a mile with Sorrow
And ne'er a word said she;
But oh, the things I learned from her
When Sorrow walked with me."
Robert Browning Hamilton

God Drills His Man
When God wants to drill a man,
And thrill a man, And skill a man
When God wants to mold a man
To play the noblest part;
When He yearns with all His heart
To create so great and bold a man
That all the world shall be amazed,
Watch His methods, watch His ways!
How He ruthlessly perfects
Whom He royally elects!
How He hammers him and hurts him,
And with mighty blows converts him
Into trial shapes of clay which
Only God understands;
While his tortured heart is crying
And he lifts beseeching hands!
How He bends but never breaks
When his good He undertakes;
How He uses whom He chooses,
And which every purpose fuses him;
By every act induces him to try His splendor out -
God knows what He's about.
Anonymous

I've Learned

rned - that you cannot make someone love you. All you can do
...meone who can be loved. The rest is up to them.

rned - that no matter how much I care, some people just don't
...ck.

rned - that it takes years to build up trust, and only seconds to
... it.

rned - that no matter how good a friend is, they're going to hurt
...ry once in a while and you must forgive them for that.

rned - that it's not *what* you have in your life but *who* you have
... life that counts.

rned - that you should never ruin an apology with an excuse.

rned - that you can get by on charm for about fifteen minutes.
...at, you'd better know something.

rned - that you shouldn't compare yourself to the best others
...

rned - that you can do something in an instant that will give you
...he for life.

rned - that it's taking me a long time to become the person I
...be.

rned - that you should always leave loved ones with loving
... It may be the last time you see them.

rned - that you can keep going long after you can't.

rned - that we are responsible for what we do, no matter how we

rned - that either you control your attitude or it controls you.

rned - that regardless of how hot and steamy a relationship is at
...e passion fades and there had better be something else to take its
...

rned - that heroes are the people who do what has to be done
... needs to be done, regardless of the consequences.

rned - that money is a lousy way of keeping score.

rned - that my best friend and I can do anything or nothing and
...e best time.

rned - that sometimes the people you expect to kick you when
...down will be the ones to help you get back up.

rned - that sometimes when I'm angry I have the right to be
...but that doesn't give me the right to be cruel.

I've learned - that true friendship continues to grow, even over the longest distance. Same goes for true love.

I've learned - that just because someone doesn't love you the way you want them to doesn't mean they don't love you with all they have.

I've learned - that maturity has more to do with what types of experiences you've had and what you've learned from them and less to do with how many birthdays you've celebrated.

I've learned - that you should never tell a child their dreams are unlikely or outlandish. Few things are more humiliating, and what a tragedy it would be if they believed it.

I've learned - that your family won't always be there for you. It may seem funny, but people you aren't related to can take care of you and love you and teach you to trust people again. Families aren't biological.

I've learned - that it isn't always enough to be forgiven by others. Sometimes you are to learn to forgive yourself.

I've learned - that no matter how bad your heart is broken the world doesn't stop for your grief.

I've learned - that our background and circumstances may have influenced who we are, but we are responsible for who we become.

I've learned - that a rich person is not the one who has the most, but is one who needs the least.

I've learned - that just because two people argue, it doesn't mean they don't love each other. And just because they don't argue, it doesn't mean they do.

I've learned - that we don't have to change friends if we understand that friends change.

I've learned - that you shouldn't be so eager to find out a secret. It could change your life forever.

I've learned - that two people can look at the exact same thing and see something totally different.

I've learned - that no matter how you try to protect your children, they will eventually get hurt and you will hurt in the process.

I've learned - that even when you think you have no more to give, when a friend cries out to you, you will find the strength to help.

I've learned - that credentials on the wall do not make you a decent human being.

I've learned - that the people you care about most in life are taken from you too soon.

I've learned - that it's hard to determine where to draw the line between being nice and not hurting people's feelings, and standing up for what you believe.

I've learned - that people will forget what you said, and people will forget what you did, but people will never forget how you made them feel.

Omer B. Washington

Smile

A smile costs nothing, but gives much. It enriches those who receive, without making poorer those who give. It takes a moment, but the memory of it sometimes lasts forever.

None is so rich or mighty that he can get along without it, and none is so poor, but that he can be made rich by it. A smile creates happiness in the home, fosters good will in business, and is the countersign of friendship. It brings rest to the weary, cheer to the discouraged, sunshine to the sad, and it is nature's best antidote for trouble. Yet it cannot be bought, begged, borrowed, or stolen, for it is something that is of no value to anyone, until it is given away.

Some people are too tired to give you a smile. Give them one of yours, as none needs a smile so much as he who has no more to give.

Anonymous

The Cookie Thief

A woman was waiting at an airport one night, with several long hours before her flight. She hunted for a book in the airport shops, bought a bag of cookies, and found a place to drop. She was engrossed in her book but happened to see that the man sitting beside her, as bold as could be, grabbed a cookie or two from the bag in between, which she tried to ignore to avoid a scene. So she munched the cookies and watched the clock, as the gutsy cookie thief diminished her stock. She was getting more irritated as the minutes ticked by, thinking, "If I wasn't so nice, I would blacken his eye."

With each cookie she took, he took one too, when only one was left, she wondered what he would do. With a smile on his face, and a nervous laugh, he took the last cookie and broke it in half. He offered her half, as he ate the other, she snatched it from him and thought . . . oooh, brother. This guy has some nerve and he's also rude, why he didn't even show any gratitude!

She had never known when she had been so galled, and sighed with relief when her flight was called. She gathered her belongings and headed to the gate, refusing to look back at the thieving ingrate.

She boarded the plane, and sank in her seat, then she sought her book, which was almost complete. As she reached in her baggage, she gasped with surprise, there was her bag of cookies, in front of her eyes.

If mine are here, she moaned in despair, the others were his, and he tried to share. Too late to apologize, she realized with grief, that she was the rude one, the ingrate, the thief.

Valerie Cox in "A Matter of Perspective"

MORAL STORIES

Encouragement From a Hospital Window

Two men, both seriously ill, occupied the same hospital room. One man was allowed to sit up in his bed for an hour each afternoon to help drain the fluid from his lungs. His bed was next to the room's only window. The other man had to spend all his time flat on his back. The men talked for hours on end. They spoke of their wives and families, their homes, their jobs, their involvement in the military service, where they had been on vacation.

Every afternoon when the man in the bed by the window could sit up, he would pass the time by describing to his roommate all the things he could see outside the window.

The man in the other bed began to live for those one-hour periods where his world would be broadened and enlivened by all the activity and color of the world outside.

The window overlooked a park with a lovely lake. Ducks and swans played on the water while children sailed their model boats. Young lovers walked arm in arm amidst flowers of every color and a fine view of the city skyline could be seen in the distance.

As the man by the window described all this in exquisite detail, the man on the other side of the room would close his eyes and imagine the picturesque scene.

One warm afternoon, the man by the window described a parade passing by. Although the other man couldn't hear the band, he could see it in his mind's eye as the gentleman by the window portrayed it with descriptive words.

Days and weeks passed.
One morning, the day nurse arrived to bring water for their baths only to find the lifeless body of the man by the window, who had died peacefully in his sleep. She was saddened and called the hospital attendants to take the body away.

As soon as it seemed appropriate, the other man asked if he could be moved next to the window. The nurse was happy to make the switch, and after making sure he was comfortable, she left him alone.

Slowly, painfully, he propped himself up on one elbow to take his first look at the real world outside.

He strained to slowly turn to look out the window beside the bed. It faced a blank wall. The man asked the nurse what could have compelled his deceased roommate who had described such wonderful things outside this window.

The nurse responded that the man was blind and could not even see the wall. She said, "Perhaps he just wanted to encourage you."

Author Unknown

Facing Difficulty
This is a real life story of engineer John Roebling building the Brooklyn Bridge in New York back in 1870. The bridge was completed in 1883, after 13 years.

In 1883, a creative engineer named John Roebling was inspired by an idea to build a spectacular bridge connecting New York with Long Island. However, bridge building experts throughout the world thought that this was an impossible feat and told Roebling to forget the idea. It just could not be done. It was not practical. It had never been done before.

Roebling could not ignore the vision he had in his mind of this bridge. He thought about it all the time and he knew deep in his heart that it could be done. He just had to share the dream with someone else. After much discussion and persuasion he managed to convince his son, Washington, an up and coming engineer, that the bridge in fact could be built.

Working together for the first time, father and son developed concepts of how it could be accomplished and how the obstacles could be overcome. With great excitement and inspiration, and the headiness of a

allenge before them, they hired their crew and began to build their
bridge.

ject started well, but when it was only a few months underway a
ccident on the site took the life of John Roebling. Washington
o injured and left with a certain amount of brain damage, which
in him not being able to talk or walk.

ld them so." "Crazy men and their crazy dreams." "It's foolish to
ild visions."

ne had a negative comment to make and felt that the project
be scrapped since the Roeblings were the only ones who knew
bridge could be built.

of his handicap, Washington was never discouraged and still had
ng desire to complete the bridge. His mind was still as sharp as
tried to inspire and pass on his enthusiasm to some of his
but they were too daunted by the task.

lay on his bed in his hospital room with the sunlight streaming
the windows, a gentle breeze blew the flimsy white curtains
d he was able to see the sky and the tops of the trees outside for
oment.

ed that there was a message for him not to give up. Suddenly an
him. All he could do was move one finger and he decided to
he best use of it. By moving this, he slowly developed a code of
nication with his wife.

hed his wife's arm with that finger, indicating to her that he
her to call the engineers again. Then he used the same method of
her arm to tell the engineers what to do. It seemed foolish but the
was under way again.

years, Washington tapped out his instructions with his finger on
e's arm, until the bridge was finally completed. Today the
ular Brooklyn Bridge stands in all its glory as a tribute to the

triumph of one man's indomitable spirit and his determination not to be defeated by circumstances. It is also a tribute to the engineers and their teamwork, and to their faith in a man who was considered mad by half the world. It stands too as a tangible monument to the love and devotion of his wife who for 13 long years patiently decoded the messages of her husband and told the engineers what to do.

Perhaps this is one of the best examples of a never-say-die attitude that overcomes a terrible physical handicap and achieves an impossible goal.

Often when we face obstacles in our day-to-day life, our hurdles seem very small in comparison to what many others have to face. The Brooklyn Bridge shows us that dreams that seem impossible can be realized with determination and persistence, no matter what the odds are.

Author Unknown

Benefits of Struggling

A man found a cocoon of a butterfly. One day, a small opening appeared. He sat and watched the butterfly for several hours as it struggled to force its body through that little hole.

Then it seemed to stop making any progress. It appeared as if it had gotten as far as it could and it could go no farther. The man decided to help the butterfly, so he took a pair of scissors and snipped off the remaining bit of the cocoon. The butterfly then emerged easily.

But it had a swollen body and small, shriveled wings. The man continued to watch the butterfly because he expected that, at any moment, the wings would enlarge and expand to be able to support the body, which would contract in time.

Neither happened! In fact, the butterfly spent the rest of its life crawling around with a swollen body and shriveled wings. It never was able to fly.

What the man in his kindness and haste did not understand was that the restricting cocoon and the struggle required for the butterfly to get through the tiny opening were God's way of forcing fluid from the body of the butterfly into its wings so that it would be ready for flight once it achieved its freedom from the cocoon.

Sometimes struggles are exactly what we need in our life. If God allowed us to go through our life without any obstacles, it would cripple us. We would not be as strong as what we could have been.

And we could never fly.

Author Unknown

Love in Action
One night, a man came to our house and told me, "There is a family with eight children. They have not eaten for days." I took some food and went to them. When I finally came to the family, I saw the faces of those little children disfigured by hunger. There was no sorrow or sadness in their faces, just the deep pain of hunger. I gave the rice to the mother. She divided it in two, and went out, carrying half the rice with her. When she came back, I asked her, "Where did you go?" She gave me this simple answer, "To my neighbors - they are hungry also."

I was not surprised that she gave - poor people are generous. But I was surprised that she knew they were hungry. As a rule, when we are suffering, we are so focused on ourselves we have no time for others.

Mother Teresa

Prison Help!
An old man lived alone in Minnesota. He wanted to spade his potato garden, but it was very hard work. His only son, who would have helped him, was in prison. The old man wrote a letter to his son and mentioned his situation:

> *Dear Son,*
>
> *I am feeling pretty bad because it looks like I won't be able to plant my potato garden this year. I hate to miss doing the garden because your mother always loved planting time. I'm just getting too old to be digging up a*

garden plot. If you were here, all my troubles would be
over. I know you would dig the plot for me, if you
weren't in prison.

Love,

Dad

Shortly, the old man received this telegram: "For Heaven's sake, Dad, don't dig up the garden!! That's where I buried the GUNS!!"

At 4 a.m. the next morning, a dozen FBI agents and local police officers showed up and dug up the entire garden without finding any guns.

Confused, the old man wrote another note to his son telling him what had happened, and asked him what to do next.

His son's reply was: "Go ahead and plant your potatoes, Dad. It's the best I could do for you, from here."

Moral: No matter where you are in the world, if you have decided to do something deep from your heart, you can do it. It is the thought that matters, not where you are or where the person is.

Author Unknown

Helpless Love
Once upon a time, all feelings and emotions went to a coastal island for a vacation. According to their nature, each was having a good time. Suddenly, a warning of an impending storm was announced and everyone was advised to evacuate the island.

The announcement caused sudden panic. All rushed to their boats. Even damaged boats were quickly repaired and commissioned for duty.

Yet, Love did not wish to flee quickly. There was so much to do. But as the clouds darkened, Love realized it was time to leave. Alas, there were no boats to spare. Love looked around with hope.

Just then Prosperity passed by in a luxurious boat. Love shouted, "Prosperity, could you please take me in your boat?"

"No," replied Prosperity, "my boat is full of precious possessions, gold and silver. There is no place for you."

A little later Vanity came by in a beautiful boat. Again Love shouted, "Could you help me, Vanity? I am stranded and need a lift. Please take me with you."

Vanity responded haughtily, "No, I cannot take you with me. My boat will get soiled with your muddy feet."
Sorrow passed by after some time. Again, Love asked for help. But it was to no avail. "No, I cannot take you with me. I am so sad. I want to be by myself."

When Happiness passed by a few minutes later, Love again called for help. But Happiness was so happy that it did not look around, hardly concerned about anyone.

Love was growing restless and dejected. Just then somebody called out, "Come Love, I will take you with me." Love did not know who was being so magnanimous, but jumped on to the boat, greatly relieved that she would reach a safe place.

On getting off the boat, Love met Knowledge. Puzzled, Love inquired, "Knowledge, do you know who so generously gave me a lift just when no one else wished to help?"

Knowledge smiled, "Oh, that was Time."

"And why would Time stop to pick me and take me to safety?" Love wondered.

Knowledge smiled with deep wisdom and replied, "Because only Time knows your true greatness and what you are capable of. Only Love can bring peace and great happiness in this world."

"The important message is that when we are prosperous, we overlook love. When we feel important, we forget love. Even in happiness and sorrow we forget love. Only with time do we realize the importance of love. Why wait that long? Why not make love a part of your life today?"

Author Unknown

Unique You

Think what a remarkable, unduplicable, and miraculous thing it is to be you! Of all the people who have come and gone on the earth, since the beginning of time, not ONE of them is like YOU!

No one who has ever lived or is to come has had or will have your combination of abilities, talents, appearance, friends, acquaintances, burdens, sorrows and opportunities.

No one's hair grows exactly the way yours does. No one's fingerprints are like yours. No one has the same combination of secret inside jokes and family expressions that you know.

The few people who laugh at all the same things you do, don't sneeze the way you do. No one prays about exactly the same concerns as you do. No one is loved by the same combination of people that love you – NO ONE!

No one before, no one to come. YOU ARE ABSOLUTELY UNIQUE!

Enjoy that uniqueness. You do not have to pretend in order to seem more like someone else. You weren't meant to be like someone else. You do not have to lie to conceal the parts of you that are not like what you see in anyone else.

You were meant to be different. Nowhere ever in all of history will the same things be going on in anyone's mind, soul and spirit as are going on in yours right now.

If you did not exist, there would be a hole in creation, a gap in history, something missing from the plan for humankind.

Treasure your uniqueness. It is a gift given only to you. Enjoy it and share it!

can reach out to others in the same way that you can. No one can
your words. No one can convey your meanings. No one can
with your kind of comfort. No one can bring your kind of
anding to another person.

can be cheerful and lighthearted and joyous in your way. No one
le your smile. No one else can bring the whole unique impact of
another human being.

our uniqueness. Let it be free to flow out among your family and
and people you meet in the rush and clutter of living wherever
. That gift of yourself was given to you to enjoy and share. Give
f away!

Receive it! Let it tickle you! Let it inform you and nudge you and
you! YOU ARE UNIQUE!

Unknown

nt Rope

an was passing the elephants, he suddenly stopped, confused by
that these huge creatures were being held by only a small rope
ne of each of their front legs. No chains, no cages. It was obvious
elephants could, at anytime, break away from their bonds, but
e reason, they did not.

a trainer nearby and asked why these animals just stood there
de no attempt to get away. "Well," the trainer said, "when they
young and much smaller we use the same size rope to tie them,
that age it's enough to hold them. As they grow up, they are
ned to believe they cannot break away. They believe the rope
ll hold them, so they never try to break free."

n was amazed. These animals could break free from their bonds
me, but because they believed they couldn't, they were stuck right
hey were.

e elephants, how many of us go through life hanging onto a belief
cannot do something, simply because we failed at it once before?

Failure is part of learning; we should never give up the struggle in life.

Author Unknown

Learn and Earn
Chuan and Jing joined a wholesale company together just after graduation. Both worked very hard.

After several years, the boss promoted Jing to sales executive but Chuan remained a sales rep. One day Chuan could not take it anymore, tender resignation to the boss and complained the boss did not value hard working staff, but only promoted those who flattered him.

The boss knew that Chuan worked very hard for the years, but in order to help Chuan realize the difference between him and Jing, the boss asked Chuan to do the following. Go, and find out if there is anyone selling watermelon in the market. Chuan returned and said, yes. The boss asked, how much per kilogram? Chuan went back to the market to ask and returned to inform the boss, $12 per kilogram.

Boss told Chuan, I will ask Jing the same question. Jing went, returned and said, boss, there is only one person selling watermelon. The price is $12 per kilogram, $100 for 10 kilograms, and he has inventory of 340 melons. On the table were 58 melons, and every melon weighed about 15 kilograms, bought from the South two days ago. They are fresh and red, good quality.

Chuan was very impressed and realized the difference between himself and Jing. He decided not to resign but to learn from Jing.

My dear friends, a more successful person is more observant, thinks more and understands in depth. For the same matter, a more successful person sees several years ahead, while you see only tomorrow. The difference between a year and a day is 365 times, how could you win? Think! How far have you seen ahead in your life? How thoughtful in depth are you?

Author Unknown

Mouse Trap

A mouse looked through the crack in the wall to see the farmer and his wife open a package. "What food might this contain?" the mouse wondered. He was devastated to discover it was a mousetrap.

Retreating to the farmyard, the mouse proclaimed the warning: "There is a mousetrap in the house! There is a mousetrap in the house!"

The chicken clucked and scratched, raised her head and said "Mr. Mouse, I can tell this is a grave concern to you, but it is of no consequence to me. I cannot be bothered by it."

The mouse turned to the pig and told him "There is a mousetrap in the house! There is a mousetrap in the house!" The pig sympathized, but said "I am so very sorry, Mr. Mouse, but there is nothing I can do about it but pray. Be assured you are in my prayers."

The mouse turned to the cow and said, "There is a mousetrap in the house! There is a mousetrap in the house!" The cow said "Wow, Mr. Mouse. I'm sorry for you, but it's no skin off my nose."

So, the mouse returned to the house, head down and dejected, to face the farmer's mousetrap alone.

That very night, a sound was heard throughout the house - like the sound of a mousetrap catching its prey. The farmer's wife rushed to see what was caught. In the darkness, she did not see it was a venomous snake whose tail the trap had caught. The snake bit the farmer's wife. The farmer rushed her to the hospital and she returned home with a fever.

Everyone knows you treat a fever with fresh chicken soup, so the farmer took his hatchet to the farmyard for the soup's main ingredient. But his wife's sickness continued, so friends and neighbors came to sit with her around the clock. To feed them, the farmer butchered the pig. The farmer's wife did not get well; she died. So many! People came for her funeral, and the farmer had the cow slaughtered to provide enough meat for all of them.

The mouse looked upon it all from his crack in the wall with great sadness. So, the next time you hear someone is facing a problem and think it doesn't concern you, remember: when one of us is threatened, we are all at risk. We are all involved in this journey called life. We must keep an eye out for one another and make an extra effort to encourage one another. Each of us is a vital thread in another person's tapestry.

What Goes Around
One day, a man saw an old lady, stranded on the side of the road, but even in the dim light of day, he could see she needed help. So he pulled up in front of her Mercedes and got out. His Pontiac was still sputtering when he approached her.

Even with the smile on his face, she was worried. No one had stopped to help for the last hour or so. Was he going to hurt her? He didn't look safe; he looked poor and hungry. He could see that she was frightened, standing out there in the cold. He knew how she felt. It was those chills which only fear can put in you. He said, "I'm here to help you, Ma'am. Why don't you wait in the car where it's warm? By the way, my name is Bryan Anderson."

Well, all she had was a flat tire, but for an old lady, that was bad enough. Bryan crawled under the car looking for a place to put the jack, skinning his knuckles a time or two. Soon he was able to change the tire. But he had to get dirty and his hands hurt. As he was tightening up the lug nuts, she rolled down the window and began to talk to him. She told him that she was from St. Louis and was only just passing through. She couldn't thank him enough for coming to her aid.

Bryan just smiled as he closed her trunk. The lady asked how much she owed him. Any amount would have been all right with her. She already imagined all the awful things that could have happened had he not stopped. Bryan never thought twice about being paid. This was not a job to him. This was helping someone in need, and God knows there were plenty, who had given him a hand in the past. He had lived his whole life that way, and it never occurred to him to act any other way.

He told her that if she really wanted to pay him back, the next time she saw someone who needed help, she could give that person the assistance they needed, and Bryan added, "And think of me." He waited until she started her car and drove off. It had been a cold and depressing day, but he felt good as he headed for home, disappearing into the twilight.

A few miles down the road the lady saw a small cafe. She went in to grab a bite to eat, and take the chill off before she made the last leg of her trip home. It was a dingy looking restaurant. Outside were two old gas pumps. The whole scene was unfamiliar to her. The waitress came over and brought a clean towel to wipe her wet hair. She had a sweet smile, one that even being on her feet for the whole day couldn't erase. The lady noticed the waitress was nearly eight months pregnant, but she never let the strain and aches change her attitude. The old lady wondered how someone who had so little could be so giving to a stranger. Then she remembered Bryan.

After the lady finished her meal, she paid with a hundred dollar bill. The waitress quickly went to get change for her hundred-dollar bill, but the old lady had slipped right out the door. She was gone by the time the waitress came back. The waitress wondered where the lady could be. Then she noticed something written on the napkin.

There were tears in her eyes when she read what the lady wrote: "You don't owe me anything. I have been there too. Somebody once helped me out, the way I'm helping you. If you really want to pay me back, here is what you do: Do not let this chain of love end with you."

Under the napkin were four more $100 bills.

Well, there were tables to clear, sugar bowls to fill, and people to serve, but the waitress made it through another day. That night when she got home from work and climbed into bed, she was thinking about the money and what the lady had written. How could the lady have known how much she and her husband needed it? With the baby due next month, it was going to be hard. She knew how worried her husband was, and as he lay sleeping next to her, she gave him a soft kiss and whispered soft and low, "Everything's going to be all right. I love you, Bryan Anderson."

There is an old saying "What goes around comes around."

(The following Parables are excerpted from Akramulla Syed's "Depression vs. Contentment.")

The Story of the Donkey in the Ditch

One day, a farmer's donkey fell into a ditch. The animal cried piteously for hours as the farmer tried to figure out what to do. Finally, he decided the animal was old, and the ditch needed to be covered up anyway; it just wasn't worth it to retrieve the donkey. He invited all his neighbors to come over and help him. They each grabbed a shovel and began to shovel dirt into the ditch. At first, the donkey realized what was happening and cried horribly. Then, to everyone's amazement, he quieted down. A few shovel loads later, the farmer looked down the ditch, and was astonished at what he saw. As every shovel of dirt hit his back, the donkey did something amazing. He would shake it off and take a step up. As the farmer's neighbors continued to shovel dirt on top of the animal, he would shake it off and take a step up. Pretty soon, everyone was amazed, as the donkey stepped up over the edge of the well and trotted off.

The Moral: My dear friends, life is going to shovel dirt on you, all kinds of dirt. The trick to getting out of the ditch is to shake it off and take a step up. Each of our troubles is a stepping-stone. We can get out of the deepest wells just by not stopping, never giving up! Shake it off and take a step up! Never lose hope and place your complete 100% trust in Almighty God as shown in the following story. A true Muslim never gives up hope in the mercy of Allah (swt), because it is a sin.

When the Winds Blow

Years ago, a farmer owned land along the Atlantic seacoast. He constantly advertised for hired hands. Most people were reluctant to work on farms along the Atlantic. They dreaded the awful storms that raged across the ocean, wreaking havoc on the buildings and crops. As the farmer interviewed applicants for the job, he received a steady stream of refusals. Finally, a short, thin man, well past middle age, approached the farmer.

you a good farmhand?" the farmer asked him. "Well, I can sleep
when the wind blows," answered the man. Although puzzled by this
reply the farmer, desperate for help, hired him. The little man worked
around the farm, busy from dawn to dusk, and the farmer felt
fied with the man's work. Then one night the wind howled loudly
from offshore. Jumping out of bed, the farmer grabbed a lantern and
ran next door to the hired hand's sleeping quarters. He shook the little
man and yelled, "Get up! A storm is coming! Tie things down before
they blow away!" The little man rolled over in bed and said firmly, "No
I told you, I can sleep when the wind blows." Enraged by the
reply, the farmer was tempted to fire him on the spot. Instead, he
went outside to prepare for the storm. To his amazement, he
discovered that all of the haystacks had been covered with tarpaulins.
Cows were in the barn, the chickens were in the coops, and the doors
were barred. The shutters were tightly secured.

thing was tied down. Nothing could blow away. The farmer then
understood what his hired hand meant, so he returned to his bed, also to
sleep while the wind blew.

Moral: My dear friends, when you're prepared, spiritually, mentally
physically, you have nothing to fear. Can you sleep when the wind
blows through your life? The hired hand in the story was able to sleep
because he had secured the farm against the storm. We with faith secure
ourselves against the storms of life by putting our trust in Almighty God,
Holy Prophet (pbuh) and his Ahlul Byat (pbut), we don't need to
understand, and we just need to hold His hand to be secure in the midst
of storms. And sleep well!

Illusion of Reflection
There was a king who had presented his daughter, the princess, with
a beautiful diamond necklace. The necklace was stolen and his people in
the kingdom searched everywhere but could not find it. Some said a bird
may have stolen it. The king then asked them all to search for it and put
a reward of $50,000 for anyone who found it.

One day, a clerk was walking home along a river next to an industrial
This river was completely polluted, filthy and smelly. As he was
walking, the clerk saw a shimmering in the river and when he looked, he

saw the diamond necklace. He decided to try and catch it so that he could get the $50,000 reward. He put his hand in the filthy, dirty river and grabbed at the necklace, but some how missed it and didn't catch it. He took his hand out and looked again and the necklace was still there. He tried again, this time he walked in the river and dirtied his pants in the filthy river and put his whole arm in to catch the necklace. But strangely, he still missed the necklace!

He came out and started walking away, feeling depressed. Then again he saw the necklace, right there. This time he was determined to get it, no matter what. He decided to plunge into the river, although it was a disgusting thing to do as the river was polluted, and his whole body would become filthy. He plunged in, and searched everywhere for the necklace and yet he failed. This time he was really bewildered and came out feeling very depressed that he could not get the necklace. Just then a saint who was walking by, saw him, and asked him what was the matter? The clerk didn't want to share the secret with the saint, thinking the saint might take the necklace for himself, so he refused to tell the saint anything. But the saint could see this man was troubled and being compassionate, again asked the clerk to tell him the problem and promised that he would not tell anyone about it. The clerk mustered some courage and decided to put some faith in the saint. He told the saint about the necklace and how he tried and tried to catch it, but kept failing. The saint then told him that perhaps he should try looking upward, toward the branches of the tree, instead of in the filthy river. The clerk looked up and true enough, the necklace was dangling on the branch of a tree. He had been trying to capture a mere reflection of the real necklace all this time.

The Moral: My dear friends, material happiness is just like the filthy, polluted river; because it is a mere reflection of the TRUE happiness in the spiritual world. We can never achieve the happiness we are looking for no matter how hard we endeavor in material life. Instead we should look upwards, toward Almighty God, who is the source of real happiness, and stop chasing after the reflection of this happiness in the material world. This spiritual happiness is the only thing that can satisfy us completely.

The Cracked Pot

Once upon a time there was a water-bearer in India who had two large pots, each hung on each end of a pole which he carried across his neck. One of the pots had a crack in it, and while the other pot was perfect and always delivered a full portion of water at the end of the long walk from the stream to the master's house, the cracked pot arrived only half full. For a full two years this went on daily, with the bearer delivering only one and a half pot full of water in his master's house. Of course, the perfect pot was proud of its accomplishments, perfect to the end for which it was made. But the poor cracked pot was ashamed of its own imperfection, and miserable that it was able to accomplish only half of what it had been made to do. After two years of what it perceived to be a bitter failure, it spoke to the water-bearer one day by the stream. "I am ashamed of myself, and I want to apologize to you." "Why?" asked the bearer. "What are you ashamed of?" "I have been able, for these past two years, to deliver only half of my load because this crack in my side causes water to leak out all the way back to your master's house. Because of my flaws, you have to do all of this work and you don't get full value from your efforts," the pot said. The water-bearer felt sorry for the old cracked pot, and in his compassion he said, "As we return to the master's house, I want you to notice the beautiful flowers along the path." Indeed, as they went up the hill, the old cracked pot took notice of the sun warming the beautiful wild flowers on the side of the path, and this cheered it some. But at the end of the trail, it still felt bad because it had leaked out half its load, and so again it apologized to the bearer for its failure. The bearer said to the pot, "Did you notice that there were flowers only on your side of your path, but not on the other pot's side? That's because I have always known about your flaw, and I took advantage of it. I planted flower seeds on your side of the path, and every day while we walk back from the stream, you've watered them. For two years I have been able to pick these beautiful flowers to decorate my master's table. Without you being just the way you are, he would not have this beauty to grace his house."

The Moral: My dear friends, each of us has our own unique flaw. But it's the cracks and flaws we each have that make our lives together so very interesting and rewarding. You've just got to take each person for what they are and look for the good in them as Holy Qur'an says:

"O you men! Surely We have created you of a male and a female, and made you tribes and families that you may know each other; surely the most honorable of you with Allah is the one among you most careful (of his duty); surely Allah is Knowing, Aware." (49:13)

And at the same time, we have to convert our flaw or weakness into strength in a positive manner, because sometimes our biggest weakness can become our biggest strength.

Converted Weakness To Strength

Take, for example, the story of one 10-year-old boy who decided to study Judo despite the fact that he had lost his left arm in a devastating car accident. The boy began lessons with an old Japanese Judo Master Sensei. The boy was doing well, so he couldn't understand why, after three months of training the master had taught him only one move.

"Sensei," the boy finally said, "Shouldn't I be learning more moves?" "This is the only move you know, but this is the only move you'll ever need to know," the Sensei replied.

Not quite understanding, but believing in his teacher, the boy kept training. Several months later, the Sensei took the boy to his first tournament. Surprising himself, the boy easily won his first two matches. The third match proved to be more difficult, but after some time, his opponent became impatient and charged; the boy deftly used his one move to win the match. Still amazed by his success, the boy was now in the finals. This time, his opponent was bigger, stronger, and more experienced. For a while, the boy appeared to be overmatched. Concerned that the boy might get hurt, the referee called a time-out. He was about to stop the match when the sensei intervened. "No," the Sensei insisted, "Let him continue." Soon after the match resumed, his opponent made a critical mistake: he dropped his guard. Instantly, the boy used his move to pin him. The boy had won the match and the tournament. He was the champion. On the way home, the boy and Sensei reviewed every move in each and every match. Then the boy summoned the courage to ask what was really on his mind. "Sensei, how did I win the tournament with only one move?" "You won for two reasons," the Sensei answered.

"First, you've almost mastered one of the most difficult throws in all of Judo. And second, the only known defense for that move is for your opponent to grab your left arm."

The Moral: My dear friends, the boy's biggest weakness had become his biggest strength.

ABOUT THE AUTHOR

Demetric Muhammad is a Student Minister, Lecturer and Researcher. His career includes more than 15 years Process Management and 8 years of Islamic Chaplaincy. His research emphasis is in the areas of Islamic Apologetics, Nation of Islam Teachings, Comparative Religions and Religion's Role In Geo-Politics. He is a Nation of Islam Gazebo Group Member.

Demetric Muhammad is also the author of *In the Light of Scripture*; *A Complete Dictionary of the Supreme Wisdom Lessons* and Who Do They Say I Am: The Vindication of Minister Louis Farrakhan.